How to Improve Your Relationship

© **Copyright 2019 - All rights reserved.**

The content contained within this book may not be reproduced, duplicated or transmitted without direct written permission from the author or the publisher.

Under no circumstances will any blame or legal responsibility be held against the publisher, or author, for any damages, reparation, or monetary loss due to the information contained within this book. Either directly or indirectly.

Legal Notice:

This book is copyright protected. This book is only for personal use. You cannot amend, distribute, sell, use, quote or paraphrase any part, or the content within this book, without the consent of the author or publisher.

Disclaimer Notice:

Please note the information contained within this document is for educational and entertainment purposes only. All effort has been executed to present accurate, up to date, and reliable, complete information. No warranties of any kind are declared or implied. Readers acknowledge that the author is not engaging in the rendering of legal, financial, medical or professional advice. The content within this book has been derived from various sources. Please consult a licensed professional before attempting any techniques outlined in this book.

By reading this document, the reader agrees that under no circumstances is the author responsible for any losses, direct or indirect, which are incurred as a result of the use of information contained within this document, including, but not limited to, — errors, omissions, or inaccuracies.

Table of Contents

Introduction..8

Chapter 1: Understanding the Value of Relationships................17

    The Marriage Contract..21

    Different Types of Relationships 25

Chapter 2: The Characteristics of a Good Relationship..............28

    Understanding the Different Types of Relationships 34

    The control relationship 35

    The open relationship 36

    The relationship of dependence (and codependency)....................37

    Sexless Relationship...39

    Long-distance relationship 40

    Friends with benefits..41

    Toxic relationships 42

    Kill time relationship...42

    Sex only relationship 43

    Love relationship 44

    Sacrificial relationship 45

    Love-hate relationship 46

Chapter 3: The Importance of Communication..........................49

    Communication Defined..50

    Communication Problems that Impact Relationships Today.............52

Listening to and Understanding Your Partner 55

Chapter 4: 10 Ways to Improve Your Communication Skills........56

Way Number One. Always be honest in your interactions with your partner. 56

Way Number Two. Know when your partner may benefit from encouragement and love. 57

Way Number Three. If you notice that you are feeling a certain way emotionally and your partner does not appear receptive, maybe this is a good time to say how you feel. 57

Way Number Four. No form of technology (even the phone) can replace face-to-face interaction. 58

Way Number Five. Schedule time that you and your partner can discuss your day. 58

Way Number Six. Know when to disconnect from media (cellphone, social media, and internet). 59

Way Number Seven. Learn how to listen rather than just hear. 59

Way Number Eight. Pay attention to the non-verbal cues that indicate how your partner is feeling. 60

Way Number Nine. Not everyone is a talker, and that's okay, but when in doubt, communicates. 60

Way Number Ten. If all else fails, consider seeing a therapist help with your communication woes. 61

Chapter 5: Emotional Intelligence...62

What Is Emotional Intelligence? 65

How to Feel and Handle Your Emotions.. 66

Fact One. Empathy is a critical part of being emotionally intelligent. .. 68

Fact Two. Research suggests that empathy is not only important in relationships but in leadership. 68

Fact Three. Emotional intelligence is a skill that can be acquired......... 69

Fact Four. Emotional intelligence is a type of intelligence similar to cognitive ability or spatial reasoning. 70

Fact Five. Individuals with emotional intelligence can use this skill in all of their relationships, not just romantic ones. 71

Fact Six. Having sympathy and having empathy is not the same thing. 72

Fact Seven. Emotional intelligence does not involve using just one ability, but several that work in tandem.. 73

Fact Eight. Individuals who lack self-regulation do not truly demonstrate emotional intelligence.. 73

Fact Nine. Non-verbal communication is an essential component of emotional intelligence as it allows us to be cued into the emotions of others. 74

Fact Ten. Active listening is an important part of empathy as well as emotional intelligence in general. 75

Chapter 6: Understanding and Overcoming Your Fears............76

Where Fear Comes From in Relationships.. 77

Overcome Your Fears by Talking... 78

Chapter 7: Couple Conflicts..80

Chapter 8: Overcoming Relationship Difficulties......................83

Chapter 9: 10 Secrets to Improving Your Relationship...............86

Secret One. Be motivated to work on your relationship. 86

Secret Two. Have empathy for your partner.. 87

Secret Three. Give your partner their own personal space. 87

Secret Four. Understand that both partners have needs in the relationship. 88

Secret Five. Recognize that in the most successful relationships, both partners see themselves as members of a team. 89

Secret Six. Love your partner, but understand that love is not always enough. 90

Secret Seven. Sometimes what's missing in a relationship is active listening. 91

Secret Eight. Recognize that people change. You are just as likely to change over time as your partner is. 91

Secret Nine. Don't be a narcissist. 92

Secret Ten. Learn to accept your partner. 92

Chapter 10: Survey: What Kind of Couple Are You? 94

100-160 points: Love relationship or Friendly couple 100

170-250 points: Love-hate relationship 101

260-320 points: Equally-matched or Twin couple 101

330-400 points: Power couple 101

Frequently Asked Questions………………………………………..102

Conclusion………………………………………………………….118

Introduction

Human beings are social animals. For this reason and others, the natural state of affairs is for individual members of the species to form relationships with other members of the species. Relationships of various kinds constitute the basis of the complex social groupings that human beings create. Relationships allow men and women to relate to one another; to form an enduring bond and to understand the proper way to interact with one another. Although a relationship does not necessarily mean love, feelings of love and of respect are implicit in most uses of the term relationship.

Indeed, one of the defining characteristics of a relationship is that it can take various shapes. This is both a reality of the different types of interactions that are necessary for human societies as well as an extension of our legacy as primates. Apes are notable among animals for their complex social interactions, and sometimes it can be helpful to study this family of creatures to understand how we as human beings function in our natural environment.

A study of apes reveals that human beings accomplish several things in relationships, including forming alliances, romantic relationships, and establishing dominance or a social hierarchy. Men and women do this in much the same way that male and female apes engage in behaviors that define and establish relationships. In fact, a study of apes reveals that many people have a simplistic view of relationships and that understanding human relationships, including why relationships fail, can benefit from going back to the basics somewhat.

What are the purposes of a relationship? Well, as the brief discourse on our primate relatives indicates, relationships help people to understand what their role in the social group is and how to relate to one another. As lifeless as that approach may seem, tackling the subject in this way can help the reader to understand the different types of relationships and why some relationships fail while others do not. Indeed, even in a romantic relationship, we can define such features as to how the pairs relate to and interact with one another emotionally, intimately, and in other ways.

Therefore, learning about relationships is important for several reasons. Learning about this subject allows men and women to understand the different types of relationships they have and how to maintain them. Maintaining relationships is not only important for functioning normally in human society, but it is important in maintaining one's sense of wellbeing. Indeed, even Maslow's hierarchy of needs recognizes relationships and attachments as a fundamental need of human beings (in the form of love and belonging).

And it is this approach to relationships as a type of need that helps understand how crucial relationships are. In his 1943 paper about human motivations, Abraham Maslow presented his theory of the needs that human beings have by virtue of being human. These needs took the form of a pyramid, at the top of which was the somewhat amorphous self-actualization, which involves an individual sense of achieving one's full potential as a human being. Other needs include food and water, shelter, safety, and esteem.

What this indicates is that forming relationships is, in its own way, as essential to human beings as food, water, shelter, being safe and secure, and having self-confidence. Because this hierarchy takes the form of a pyramid, basic physiologic needs (like food, shelter, and water) must be met first while other essential needs are addressed once these basic ones have been met. Relationships – as part of a need for love and belonging – are on the third step of the five-step pyramid, sitting right in the middle of this construction of human needs: both literally and figuratively.

Indeed, forming the right sorts of relationships can be important for happiness and success in life. Relationships are a central feature of our existence as human beings, and devoting time to understanding them and improving them can result in a dramatic change in the quality of life. Many books have been written on how to win friends and how to be successful at business, and nearly all of these books focus on one thing: forming the right relationships and using them to your advantage.

Although this book does not approach the subject from the standpoint of business, this way of thinking can help readers to understand the sorts of purposes that relationships serve. It may seem strange to think of a relationship in terms of a deal or a business agreement of some kind, but this is basically the sort of purpose that various types of relationships serve. They are essentially a lot of sorts between you and another person: an agreement that defines what the relationship is for.

For example, a friendship may be seen as being something jovial between two individuals that are fond of each other, but it comes with some expectations. If I, as a friend, make an appointment to meet, I expect you to show up. If I, as a friend, lend you a certain sum of money I expect you to pay me back and to be available to lend me money in the future if I ever need it. I, as a friend, expect you not to make moves on my girlfriend or boyfriend and you can expect me not to do the same to your boyfriend or girlfriend. The idea here is that all relationships actually serve a purpose and are defined by often specific sets of expectations.

The intention of this book is not, in fact, to focus on how to use your relationships to get rich or win friends but to use knowledge of this important human bond to improve your relationship. We focus on the romantic relationship and the many subtypes that fall within the guise of this type of relationship. Learning about the basic nature of relationships and specifically about various aspects of romantic relationships allows men and women to understand what the characteristics of a good relationship are and, perhaps, why some of them may be problematic.

Relationships have value, and understanding this is the first step toward maintaining your important relationships and establishing good ones. The value of relationships has been studied extensively in psychology and behavioral biology. At its most basic level, relationships evolved because they served an essential function in primate societies and the existence of these types of bonds enhanced survival. In the first chapter, a holistic definition of the relationship will be defined and different types of relationships will be explored.

There are certain characteristics that help to define a good relationship. At the same time, there are certain aspects of the relationship that help you know whether or not this union is important in your life. As we have seen, relationships serve a basic purpose, which means that certain of them, you may have an interest in preserving. In the second chapter, we will not only explore further the different types of relationships that men and women can develop with their partners, but we will also come to understand better what the characteristics of good, important relationships are.

Another aspect of human behavior that is often taken for granted is communication. Indeed, communication is the basic currency that allows relationships to happen. Relationships can be of a purely sexual or physical nature; however, relationships that do not have good communication at a basic level often fail. The purpose of the third chapter is to help the reader understand the importance of communication and how to improve communication. Because communication can be both verbal and non-verbal (and both of these are enormously important in human interaction), the third chapter will explore how readers can work on both of these aspects of communication. The reader will also be provided with the tools they need to help them to listen and understand their partner.

Indeed, improving your communication skills is one of the quickest and easiest things that you can do to improve your communication. Although human beings are naturally imbued with the skills to interact with one another, verbally and non-verbally, both social and individualistic factors can serve as impediments to good communication. Communication problems can stem from dysfunctional relationships with one's parents during childhood, or they can be an extension of all the muck that comes from the digital age in which we live.

This means that your communication skills (or lack thereof) may not be fully your fault. It is important to be able to say *mea culpa*, but in some cases, the fact of the matter is *mea no culpa*. It may not be your fault. That does not mean that there are no steps that you can take to fix some of the relationship issues in your life. In the fourth chapter, we list ten of the major ways that you can better communicate and, by extension, improve your relationship.

Like everything else in life, relationships are a two-way street. You play a role in the success or failure of your relationship just as much as your partner does. This is one of the important aspects of relationships and of communication: it takes two to tango. This is part of the reason why emotional intelligence is important. Like the relationship itself, emotional intelligence involved because it, in important ways, helped to enhance the chances of human survival.

Emotional intelligence refers to a host of skills that human beings utilize to engage in communication with one another. These skills include well-known things like self-awareness and empathy, but they also include abilities such as self-regulation and emotion-guided behavior, which are also essential to having a good relationship. In the fifth chapter, issues of emotional intelligence that are relevant to relationships will be explored. This includes defining emotional intelligence and introducing the emotional intelligence skills that can be essential to have a happy life and healthy relationships.

Much of the problems that men and women have with relationships stem from various types of problems that people experience as a result of their upbringing. Men and women may have fears that influence their ability to interact with others and form relationships. This makes overcoming fear an important aspect of improving and maintaining relationships. In the sixth chapter, the importance of understanding and overcoming fears and living in the moment will be explored.

Some people have fears about the conflict in a relationship. These are often legitimate fears that stem from prior problems with relationships in the past, or from real problems that currently exist in a relationship. These fears can permeate into a relationship and cause conflict. Although this is one of several potential sources of conflict, it is an important one. In the seventh chapter, we will review the main reasons for conflict in a relationship.

The next step then becomes how to overcome these sorts of difficulties in a relationship. It is significant to recognize her that your own fears can work in tandem with the fears of your partner to create a relationship that is characterized by emotions (and their results) that you and your partner may not be in full control of. Once this is recognized, steps can be taken by you and your partner to work toward the improvement of your bond. This effort includes basic but important steps like recognizing personal space, allowing your partner to have time unto themselves. It is also important here to remember communication. Sharing your feelings and experiences with your partner is an important way of infusing empathy (part of emotional intelligence) into your relationship.

Many books on relationships focus on the tricks that you can use to work magic on your union. Although this book's primary focus is on education, we do recognize that some people learn better with information delivered in easily-digestible particles. In the ninth chapter, we focus on the secrets that you can use to improve your relationship. These secrets are called such because they are often overlooked by men and women, although they can be rather effective in working things out.

Lastly, some men and women in relationships have the basic problem of recognizing the kind of relationship they have. It is often easy to acknowledge the sort of relationship that is wanted, but understanding what reality often requires an outsider looking in. It is not always easy to take a step outside of oneself to really see what is going on, as someone who is an observer would be able to. The first two chapters will explore the different types of relationships while the purpose of the tenth chapter is to help the reader narrow down which types their own relationship falls into. This will be undertaken in the form of a survey which asks the question, *what kind of couple are you*?

Equipped with these tools, you will not only be able to take steps towards saving your relationship but will ask (and answer) the basic question of whether your relationship is worth saving. If you are reading this, then most likely your bond is one that you want to keep. It is not impossible to accomplish this, but it will take some work on the part of you and your partner, and all this begins with a little education.

Chapter 1: Understanding the Value of Relationships

Relationships are of such importance to human beings that multiple fields within social science concern themselves with describing and studying them. Sociologists study the various interpersonal relationships that characterize human social groups. Anthropologists study the individual variations in relationships and relationship formation that exist across societies. Psychologists study how problems in relationships can manifest in the form of mental disorders or unhappiness.

The question, of course, becomes why does relationships have such great value to humans? Human beings are capable of thinking and behaving autonomously and therefore, should not require the sort of support that relationships represent. The significance of relationships (as observed and studied by social scientists) implies that human beings may not be as self-sufficient as they like to think. Human adults can meet their own needs for food, shelter, and water. We can be responsible for meeting our own needs for safety and security. Even our sense of self-confidence and esteem stems essentially from qualities within ourselves.

Perhaps the simplest way to understand the value of relationships comes from analyzing our closest relatives: the chimpanzees. Chimpanzees share 97% of our DNA. These apes have been studied extensively, as have other primates like gorillas. These animals have been shown to experience much the same range of emotions as human beings. They feel sadness and loneliness. When they are scared, they comfort each other. When they are exposed to painful stimuli, they release the stress hormone cortisol, just like human beings do. When one ape in a long-term relationship dies, it has been observed that sometimes another ape perishes not long afterward. Clearly, as different as we like to suppose that we are from our primate cousins, relationships play an important role in the fabric of their lives just as they do in us.

In truth, relationships serve an essential function for human beings. This function can be understood by taking a look at Abraham Maslow's hierarchy of needs. The hierarchy of needs represents the basic requirements that individuals must meet in order to be stable and happy. Essentially this hierarchy represents the human quality of life, for without, our men our women will feel dissatisfaction, depression, and if their basic needs are not met, they may even experience death. The hierarchy exists in the form of a pyramid at the bottom of which are the basic needs of food, shelter, and water, and at the top of which is self-actualization: one's need to achieve one's full potential as a human being (or at least to feel that one has done so). Sitting right in the middle of this pyramid is love and belonging.

Relationships fill the need that human beings have for love and belonging. It may be strange to think of it this way by psychologists and other social scientists regard these needs as practically as essential as food, water, shelter, security, and safety. In other words, feeling love and belonging that comes from a relationship with another (or others) is essential to our survival. What Maslow's hierarchy of needs does is help us to understand how human beings can be both a species with the individual will and a group that requires close interaction with others.

We use the term relationship to describe the wide variety of bonds that human beings form with one another. These bonds take the form of the sorts of partnerships that most readers have experienced in their own lives. You will have formed attachments to your parents, siblings, aunts and uncles, and other close members of your family. In childhood and through to adulthood, you likely formed a friendship with others based on common interests or shared personality traits. You formed romantic relationships based on sexual attraction or the subjective feeling of love.

Although any enduring interaction between two people can be described as a relationship, romantic relationships are the focus of this book. Here we are talking about serious romantic relationships. These do not have to exist in the form of marriage, but typically relationships of the sort that this book deals with are akin to marriage. Partners feel love and respect for one another, even if those feelings have not been solemnized in the form of a marriage document.

Many readers will be reading this book because they recognize that their relationship is flawed or because they have an interest perhaps in avoiding the sorts of mistakes that they have made in this. One of the points that this book attempts to get across is that there are certain qualities associated with all good or important relationships, regardless of whether or not these relationships involve sex. If we approach relationships from the standpoint of basic human needs, then we can often understand why partners in relationships may struggle or why the union may even fail.

So understanding your own relationship problems requires that you first understand what a relationship is and why it is. We have defined a relationship as an enduring interaction between two or more people. We can go on further to say that this enduring interaction, by definition serves an important function for all parties involved. If we return to the hierarchy of needs, we can remind the reader that relationships meet the basic need that human beings have for love and belonging.

Relationships can arise in many different ways. Although it is not the intention of this book to cause you to question how or why your present romantic relationship arose, it is often the case that relationships arise for what we might call the wrong reasons. These bad reasons for a relationship can often manifest in the form of relationship dysfunction. For example, two people who work together and are competitive may end up getting married or becoming serious partners. But because their relationship has a competitive or even adversarial quality, they may find themselves in what we would call a love-hate relationship.

Therefore, though the question of how you entered into a relationship with your partner is almost peripheral to the conversation, this question can crop up into the type of bond your relationship develops into. Discussing relationship type is an important exercise because it helps you to understand the sort of relationship that you are in, particularly in terms of a web of symptoms or problems. That is not to say that every relationship type has some element of dysfunction, but many of them do.

Indeed, many relationship types have been named, studied, and described because they exhibit some particular flaw that eats away at the relationship until it is gone.

The Marriage Contract

Before we get into the different types of relationships, it is important to return to the role that these bonds form in human society. And this is really what they are: bonds, even if they are not necessarily set in stone in the form of legal documentation. We have explored the idea that human beings as primates naturally form bonds with others of their species and that these bonds serve an important evolutionary function. We have also seen that the formation of these bonds satisfies an essential need that human beings have. But the role that relationships serve may become even more obvious by performing a sort of anthropological study of bonds (namely, marriages) in the West.

Western anthropologists often find themselves journeying to isolated islands in the Pacific or to distant villages in Africa in an attempt to describe how the people live. They do this out of curiosity – to help to expand the database of human knowledge – but they also do this because they hope to understand human beings better. When all is said and done, there are certain qualities that human beings have that persist across society.

One characteristic that has endured throughout Man's time on Earth has been the marriage. Societies from one corner of the world to other form marriages, usually solemnized by a priest or a holy man. Evidence going back thousands of years suggests that humans have long united in the form of the marriage bond. There have even been discoveries dating back tens of thousands of years of male and female skeletons buried side by side in a sort of lover's embrace.

It is therefore easy for us to look at other groups and use them as clues to understanding ourselves as human beings better. But sometimes, it is useful to turn that high-powered lens on ourselves. Throughout Western European history, there has existed something called the marriage contract. Now, the purpose of this book is not to focus on marriage, but it is important to acknowledge that many people choose to put an official stamp on their relationship by becoming married, and in some societies, marriage may be the only socially acceptable way for two individuals to have an enduring romantic relationship.

Marriage contracts have been found dating back to ancient times. In Ancient Rome, citizens were capable of engaging in different types of marriage: one of which was preserved for patricians and had a particularly serious, quasi-religious function. Even if the expectation in these sorts of marriages was that the two partners would not break the union in the form of divorce, there was nearly always a marriage contract of sorts which identified who was responsible for bringing what to the marriage, and who would be taking what should the marriage be dissolved.

This marriage contract endured right up to recent times, and some may even consider the prenuptial agreement as to the modern equivalent of the marriage contract. What the marriage contract accomplished (and what the prenup does) is specifies who has what and who is entitled to what in the marriage. Today, this is done more for convenience (and with the knowledge that the two parties may one day decide to separate their union), but in the past, this sort of contract was just as important as any other contract.

The marriage contract had such importance because a marriage then was not merely the union of two people who loved each other or had a deep attraction for one another. Marriage was a union between two families. Indeed, in certain parts of the world, marriage still forms this function. Although this sort of arrangement may seem to cheapen marriage or to ignore the feelings of the individuals being married, what the marriage contract did was recognize the value this relationship had and to take measures to ensure its survival.

Indeed, the marriage contract (unlike the prenup) was not designed to irritate the married individuals by forcing them to think about money and other assets when their thoughts are really ones of love. The purpose of the marriage contract was to appease both families by making all the financial ins and outs of the marriage clear from the very beginning. What the marriage contract did was make marriages more likely to endure by removing financial assets as a source of marriage conflict. As we will see later, issues of financial honesty and equity can be a major source of conflict in a marriage.

So what is the purpose of talking about marriage contracts in the context of relationships? Well, let's face it. Most people in the West today enter into serious romantic relationships because they "love" the other person, or at least feel a strong sexual attraction towards them. Again, there isn't necessarily anything wrong with that. Issues with modern relationships may come about because there is not a mutual recognition on the purpose that the relationship serves for both parties, and because love just may not be enough to keep marriages going. As many readers can attest, sometimes love fades. Or perhaps you may find yourself more in love with someone else.

But what a marriage contract does, at least in a financial sense, is to state the expectations that both parties have regarding the relationship. I, as a partner in the marriage, need this and expect this. In return, I will give the other party this and that. For example, a Renaissance marriage contract may require Signore So and So – the father of the bride - to provide a dowry of 8,000 ducats for his daughter, but in return Signore Bada Bing – the groom – would set aside some of his own property for the upkeep of the bride and promised to return the dowry to the bride's father if the bride should pass without children.

Although there is something sterile and dehumanizing about this sort of contract, it does acknowledge that an aspect of relationships is the respective needs of the concerned parties. If we leave aside the marriage contract and think about other needs that men and women may have in a relationship, we can say that some needs include things like emotional support, love, close physical proximity, sex, and even safety and security, which represent their own separate rung on the hierarchy of needs.

What men and women do today is failing to recognize that relationships come with a series of needs for both parties, and that love is just one of those needs. Because there is such a focus on love, men and women in relationships often ignore that their relationships often serve other functions. It is not until these other needs or functions are not being met that people often become aware of them as they pop up in the form of conflicts. For example, a couple may marry for "love", but then they wind up in divorce proceedings when one of the partners loses their employment or source of income.

It becomes useful then to think about your relationship in terms of your needs that are being met by the relationship as well as your partner's needs. Although no one likes to think about the financial aspects of relationships, serious romantic partnerships have a need for safety and security and financial security is part and parcel of that. In fact, some individuals may fall out of love but stay together solely because there is a financial component to the relationship that they need.

Different Types of Relationships

Once the understanding is gained that a relationship meets essential needs of both parties and that a review of these needs is often essential in analyzing relationship conflict a discussion can be had on the different types of relationships. As stated previously, not all of these delineated relationship types are dysfunctional, but most of them are. This is because many studies on relationships focus on problems in relationships, so there is a lot of terminology about problem areas.

Every relationship is different. That being said, thinking about relationships in terms of types can help you develop a general gestalt for the spectrum of problems that may characterize your particular relationship. Just as one may be careful with stereotypes as they are often not true, one must also be careful to see all of the aspects of relationship types as applying to you or your relationship. Indeed, you may find that your relationship has characteristics of two or more different types.

There are several methods of dividing relationships into types. Here, we focus on a practical division that emphasizes the salient characteristics of that relationship. This may seem like reducing something as complex as a relationship into a simple label like "sexless" or "love-hate" and it is, but it is necessary to do this for the reasons already mentioned. Some types of relationships may not be mentioned here or may have alternative names that we have used instead.

Here is a list of the relationship types that will be explored in the next chapter:

- The control relationship
- The open relationship
- The relationship of dependence
- Sexless Relationship
- Long-distance relationship
- Friends with benefits
- Toxic relationships
- Kill time relationship
- Sex only relationship
- Love relationship
- Sacrificial relationship

- Love-hate relationship

Some of these will be familiar to readers. The long-distance relationship is one of the most common types of romantic partnerships, even if it does not necessarily imply an inherent dysfunction in the nature of the relationship. Again, there is a variation in terminology that can be applied to these relationship types, so the dependent relationship is often referred to as codependency in psychological literature even though it refers to the same thing.

Your relationship is just as unique as you are so you should not allow yourself to be constrained by a label, but such labels can help you and your partner identifies some of the key problems areas in your union.

Chapter 2: The Characteristics of a Good Relationship

Relationships exist because they serve an important function for human beings. Unfortunately, not all relationships accomplish the tasks that we associate with relationships. A relationship should not only meet your needs as an individual and as a partner, but you should feel happy, confident, and fulfilled in your relationship. Feeling happy, confident, and fulfilled is actually a recognition that a relationship is meeting your needs: that you are in a good relationship. Indeed, sometimes the best way to think about the characteristics of a good relationship is to discuss bad ones and tell people that their relationship should be the opposite of that.

For better or worse, individuals in a relationship often bring their own personal issues or baggage into the partnership. Most of the time, this is not a conscious decision on the part of the baggage-bringer but a byproduct of the dysfunctional upbringing that person experienced and sometimes the personality disorder that resulted. Indeed, personality disorders and other aspects of mental illness can be such a dysfunction in terms of relationships that psychologists and psychologists have extensively studied them. These professionals study these people because they seek to understand how problems in development can manifest themselves in problems during adulthood. In general, attachment problems in childhood lead to problems forming or functioning normally in relationships.

A particular disorder and personality trait that is oft written and spoken of is that of the narcissist. Indeed, of all of the psychiatric disorders for which there are books available for download today, few have gotten the attention that narcissistic personality disorder has gotten. The narcissist has even given the anxious or depressed person a run for their money when it comes to books targeted at them. Of course, the book about narcissists is generally written from the standpoint of how those around the narcissist (or in a relationship with the narcissist) can best handle them.

The narcissist is an extremely vain individual who does not see the needs or concerns of others as being equal to their own. They regard themselves as special people who deserve special consideration, and they use their great awareness of others to manipulate them into giving them what they want. A narcissist will even tear down the self-esteem of another because it is essential in reinforcing their own vanity. Narcissists are also codependent in that, though they may demean their partner, they actually need their partner there to enable and support their narcissistic tendencies.

Codependency is something that will be explored in a minute, but it is important to focus here on the fact that the relationship with the narcissist represents perhaps the worst sort of relationship that one person can have with another. Though a narcissist is emotionally aware (both of their own emotions and those of their partner), they do not experience empathy generally because they do not regard the feelings of others as being equal or equivalent to their own and therefore are unable to care deeply for others. The narcissist will never care as much about others as they care about themselves.

This represents a problem in a relationship because it means that only the needs of the narcissist are being met as those are the only needs that matter in the relationship, at least from their point of view. Indeed, as callous and harmful as the narcissist may seem (and is), they still have needs that fall along Maslow's hierarchy of needs and which are being satisfied in the relationship. For example, the need for love and attachment plays out in the narcissist's codependency, even though it means that they demean and coerce their partner into staying close.

Therefore, in a relationship with a narcissist, most of the characteristics of a good, healthy, or important relationship are absent. Even communication can be said to be absent as the narcissist is so manipulative that conversing with them is characterized by dishonesty, ulterior motives, and an overall falseness that prevents the communication from having any real meaning to anyone except the narcissist.

Of course, there are types of bad relationships that do not quite approach the level of the union with the narcissist. Individuals who are highly emotional or who experiences vagaries of love and hate can also be extremely problematic to have a relationship with. Although these individuals are perhaps not as sinister as the narcissist, they also have a personality disorder that prevents them from having normal interactions with others because of their own dysfunction. People like this experienced confused emotions as children, so they developed a pattern of confusing emotions as adults: feeling love one moment, hate the next moment, and lust the moment after that, all because they did not experience accurate emotional sensitization from their parents.

Although it is not the point here to say that all bad relationships come from mental disorders, it is important to acknowledge that these sorts of problems can certainly manifest in a relationship. Indeed, many books have been written on how depressed or anxious individuals can manifest symptoms of their illness in the context of a relationship. Steps need to be taken both by the depressed or anxious individual and by their partner to salvage the relationship.

In reality, it is almost a cop-out to attribute relationship problems to mental illness. Sure, narcissists, bipolar, or borderline people may be nearly impossible to have a good relationship with (if they are no on the treatment of some kind), but they do not represent the entirety of bad partners. Let's face it, some people are just not the nicest or not the easiest to deal with and this can manifest itself in a relationship. Many psychologists would say that people like this have a dysfunctional personality trait (if not an actual disorder) although this still seems to absolve the bad partner of guilt.

In the end, we can almost say that it does not matter why the bad partner is a bad partner. They may have a mental illness or they may not have one. Your position as the other in your relationship is to try and figure out the problems so that you can fix them and potentially turn your relationship into a good one. So as much as it is interesting to explore the ins and outs of the relationship with the narcissist or borderline person, it is more important to examine how we can recognize particular relationship problems or conflicts and make the determination that they can be fixed or not.

So, now that we are done with the narcissistic relationship (at least for now) we can spend a moment to talk about what makes relationships good. A point that we will continue to drive home throughout this book is that a good or important relationship is one in which the needs of both partners are being met. Such relationships are characterized by love. Both partners feel love for one another, rather than lust. This love represents that these individuals have formed a serious attachment to one another, and their relationship is part and parcel of that attachment.

As we will see in a moment, it is important to make the distinction between love and lust. These are often confused, especially in the modern age where there does seem to be a lot of emphases placed on the sexual aspect of relationships. Of course, sex has always been an important part of relationships (or else none of us would be here), but it has become increasingly common for relationships to be formed solely for the purposes of sex. Relationships like these are often formed on the basis of sexual attraction or lust, rather than love.

Now, the purpose of this discussion is not to debase attraction as an important player in human relations with one another. Although there has been an almost reactionary movement to construct sexual attraction as inherently bad, it is actually natural for human beings to be sexually attracted to one another. Lust is definitely a loaded word – burdened with Judeo-Christian assumptions about motives and the subjective goodness or badness of them – but if we think about lust in terms of sexual attraction, it becomes perhaps easier to analyze it.

For example, a married man may feel sexually attracted to a woman he sees walking down the street, but he may also be sexually attracted to his wide, even if she is dressed in the proverbial potato sack. By the same token, a woman may be attracted to the slim-waisted hunk on the beach, but she may also be sexually attracted to her husband, even if he has a "Dad bod." The sexual attraction is not necessarily bad. Indeed, sexual attraction can be a powerful force to keep two individuals together. It may even be the primary motivator for a relationship.

But at the end of the day, sexual attraction is not to love. This becomes obvious if you take a moment to think about all the people in your life that you love. Perhaps you love your father and mother; perhaps you love your brothers and sisters. Maybe you would say you love someone at work that you have been working with for a long time or other people in your life that you are not necessarily in a serious relationship with. You can love anyone, and that love can exist both inside a romantic relationship and outside of one.

Love is an important component of a good relationship, just like the sense that a partner has that their needs are being satisfied. Another important component, actually related to love, is acceptance. Acceptance means that one partner is able to accept the other for who he or she is, without feeling the need to change them. Although it is only natural when you love someone that you want to see them happy and successful, acceptance means that you take that person for who they are, even those things that you may not always like about them (like their beard or their weight).

It is easy to see why acceptance is an important part of love. Indeed, some would argue that love is acceptance. Acceptance is almost like a marriage vow: for richer or poorer, through sickness and health. You are willing to take the other person as they are with the knowledge that they will, in turn, take you as you are. When you truly love someone and are committed to a relationship with them (romantic or not), you can accept them and have them, in turn, accept you. This type of interaction is practically an emotional one: mutual acceptance forms a bond that takes two people and makes them one.

Understanding the Different Types of Relationships

Hopefully, at this point, you have a better sense of the sorts of things that make a good relationship or a bad one. Now we can start to think about the different types of relationships and how they show signs of good or bad relationships. As stated previously, most of these relationship types are bad ones because people tend to spend time focusing on problems in relationships and why they exist rather than the variations of a good relationship. As Tolstoy famously said in his opening line to Anna Karenina: "All happy families are alike; every unhappy family is unhappy in its own way."

So, let us take a moment to try and figure out why your unhappy family is so. It is easy to fall into the trap of blaming oneself for the problems that can manifest in a relationship, but it is important to note that both partners typically contribute to the problems that surface in a relationship. Even something as simple as not responding well to something your partner does that aggravates you represents a failure on the part of both people. With that said, individuals with certain personality disorders, like a narcissistic personality disorder, often use a blame game to psychology break down their partner so we want to approach this subject neutrally. Approach these relationship types as an outsider, not as someone looking to blame themselves as the problem partner.

The control relationship

A relationship should be characterized by love, acceptance, and respect. These qualities represent a measure of equality or equivalence in a relationship. For example, respect is something that partners have for each other. If one partner respects the other but this is not reciprocated, then the relationship may run into problems. The control relationship is notable for lack of equality. One partner attempts to control, manipulate, or dictate the actions of the other person. This control may be a conscious attempt by one partner to "rule over" the other person or it may be part of a psychiatric disorder in which the controller feels a need for this type of dynamic.

As with narcissistic individuals, the controller in this relationship may not see the desires or feelings of the other person as being equal to their own.

A relationship of control implies that the needs or the desires of one person are regarded as more important than the needs or desires of the other, which indicates a fundamental lack of respect or equality between the two partners. Although some partners may respect the controller in the relationship and may not personally have a problem with being the secondary partner in the relationship, this type of dynamic can lead to problems because the needs of one person are not being met. Recall that a relationship should fill basic human needs that both partners have.

The open relationship

Indeed, the ideal relationship meets the needs of both individuals rather than merely one. The major problem with the control relationship is a problem that underlies many of the relationships mentioned here. These fundamentally unequal relationships eventual lead to problems, especially as Western society has moved towards a more egalitarian view of life: where the needs and views of all are treated equally. The open relationship can be said to represent a particularly egalitarian relationship, but it is also one fraught with difficulties.

In the open relationship, there is often a spoken or unspoken rule that both partners are permitted to have other romantic partners or lovers even in the context of what the two original partners regard as a serious relationship. Of course, it seems strange to some that two people could have a serious relationship and still have casual sexual encounters with other persons. These encounters with others may even be ongoing. But the idea behind an open relationship is that the partners are able to satisfy their sexual needs with people other than their partners.

The open relationship is a modern label for a structure that has existed in various forms throughout history. Polyandrous or polygamous relationships may appear garish to some but they are not as rare or unusual as people may think. For example, in aristocratic circles in France before the Revolution, it was common for both men and women in a marriage to have lovers. Even modern presidents of France have been honored at their funerals by their wives and mistresses standing side by side. The problem with the open relationship is obvious – that one or both partners may become jealous and this can cause friction in the relationship – but there are many men and women around the world who are able to make this arrangement work for them. The question becomes how can partners meet their respective needs and whether the relationship is able to accomplish this.

The relationship of dependence (and codependency)

Dependence is a concept that can be a source of confusion for some. Dependence can be confused with codependence, which is a particularly problematic relationship dynamic that is often associated with personality disorders. The relationship of dependence refers to partners who are together because they depend on each other to meet essential needs, like food and shelter, as opposed to the more abstract needs for love, acceptance, and contentment that characterize healthier relationships. We, therefore, need to distinguish this dependence relationship from codependence, which will be described shortly.

The idea that two partners in a relationship may depend on one another for the satisfaction of their needs is not particularly odd, but codependence refers to a situation in which demeaning behavior, emotional abuse, or even other types of abuse or used to keep one individual in a relationship. The abusive person engages in this sort of behavior because they actually need the person whom they seem to be abusing.

Codependence really represents true dependence on the one hand and invented dependence on the other. In other words, one partner needs the other while the other partner only thinks they need their other half. In the case of narcissists, who commonly demonstrate codependence, the narcissist uses manipulative strategies to create the belief in their partner that they need the narcissist, while they often do not. This is especially true as the narcissist can be so self-centered and self-interested as they are unlikely to meet needs outside of their own. Therefore it is the narcissist who needs the degraded partner, while the degraded partner only thinks that they need the narcissist.

It is obvious why this type of relationship is unhealthy. This is a relationship characterized by manipulation and dishonesty, which are stressors on a relationship. One cannot meet one's own needs for esteem, safety, and security in a relationship where one is being manipulated and lied to, and where emotions expressed are generally false and manipulative in nature. This is a relationship in which the needs of the secondary partner are not being met, so if they were to ever develop esteem (as human beings are meant to), they would naturally incline to leave the relationship.

Sexless Relationship

The sexless relationship may be more common than people realize. It is common in the Western society of today to associate the term relationship with love and sex (of which the distinctions between the two are not always clear). Most people today see love as an essential component of a relationship, and for many people, this means sex. But if one thinks about the purpose of a relationship, like a bond that meets the needs of the involved partners, this purpose does not necessarily include sex. Indeed, although some consider sex to be an essential component of a normal human life, this is not generally thought of as a need that human beings must-have.

The question of whether or not sex is essential for individuals to be happy is a loaded one. Sex is definitely a normal part of life, even if some religions or religious groups may have a pathological approach to sex. Sex is also necessary for procreation. But if we think about the roles that relationships have in human societies, they are not always about procreation. You have relationships with your parents, siblings, and friends and these (hopefully) do not involve a secret desire for procreation. All jokes aside, even a romantic relationship can be a stable, healthy, and meaningful one without sex.

This type of relationship is not necessarily a "bad" one though it can be. This relationship can be problematic if one partner feels that they have a need for sex and the other partner does not have the same need or even has an aversion towards sex. Sex aversions are relatively common, particularly in women, so sexless relationships often result. Again, this type of relationship does not have to be problematic. A general rule is that relationship features become problematic when the needs of one or both partners are not being met.

Long-distance relationship

The long-distance relationship is an increasingly common type of partnership. Although not new, the ease of travel and technological advancements in communication has made the long-distance relationship more prevalent than ever before. As the name implies, this relationship is characterized by partners who live some distance from one another. This distance means that close physical contact is often rare in the relationship, and communication often happens via phone, email, text, or video chat.

Long-distance relationships can work. This type of relationship is not being discussed here because there is something inherently dysfunctional about it. But as partners in a relationship often have a need for physical closeness, sex, or even the sense of security that physical proximity can provide, long-distance relationships have stressors that are generally absent from other relationship types. Because every relationship is different in terms of the needs that the bond fills for its members, many couples are able to do fine being apart from one another. Long-distance relationships generally involve some periods of closeness, which allows the needs men and women have related to closeness to be met at these times.

Friends with benefits

Friends with benefits describe a relationship that is essentially a friendship but has components of the romantic relationship. Romantic relationships generally have, if not actual sex, some element of physical contact or intimacy that differentiates that type of relationship from other types, like friendships or familial relationships. Friends with benefits developed as a tongue in cheek term to describe these types of unions where friends were physically intimate with one another on occasion, with the implication being that the intimacy met the physical needs that the friends had.

The term friends with benefits carry with it a lot of connotations, some of which may not be wholly accurate. Friends with benefits are often thought of as people who should be in a committed romantic relationship but lack the maturity or interest in pursuing a partnership of that type. Some think of friends with benefits in terms of people who are promiscuous and are looking for an almost healthy outlet for their promiscuity.

In reality, friends with benefits represent a type of relationship that can be both a friendship and a romantic relationship. In other words, this relationship is more than just a friendship with sex. Therein lies the problem. Friends with benefits relationships often fail because one person sees the bond as a friendship while the other person sees it as a romantic relationship. Therefore, one person may not be jealous or upset if the other is intimate with someone else, while the other may be hurt if the situation was reversed. These relationships can be dangerous because most people are not able to navigate the pitfalls that come from adding sex to an essentially non-sexual relationship. The sex dimension often sabotages not only the sexual relationship but the original friendship.

Toxic relationships

The toxic relationship is just what it sounds like. It is a relationship that is so dysfunctional, so fraught with inherently dangerous and damaging actions that it becomes toxic to everyone involved. A toxic relationship is really a general term that can describe many different types of relationships. A relationship may be toxic because one partner is a manipulative narcissist, or it may be toxic because it is a love-hate relationship characterized by passionate sex and mutual antipathy outside of sex. Even a sexless relationship can be toxic if the partners feel that sex is necessary for them and they are dying without it.

The toxic relationship is damaging enough that the partners in it are hurt just by virtue of being a part of it, and generally, it is better if they decide to end it. Although even the most dysfunctional relationships covered here can sometimes be salvaged, the toxic relationship is the example of one that is best to get out of it as quickly as you can.

Kill time relationship

Relationships are a normal way for human beings to relate to one another. That is why they are called relationships. For this reason, some people enter into unions because they need to be with someone, either for keeping up appearances sake or because of codependency reasons, which can lead to a kill time relationship. The kill time relationship is a partnership that exists just to meet the superficial needs that a relationship can serve, which includes being able to tell others that you are in a relationship and having something to do to "kill time."

Although a kill time relationship is certainly not a toxic one, this type of partnership does not meet the sort of essential needs that a relationship often serves. These relationships are not characterized by intimacy, respect, acceptance, or even love. These are relationships in name only. Marriage can even be described as a kill time relationship if the partners do not experience emotional or physical closeness to one another. A kill time relationship frequently ends when one partner discovers that they have needs that their partner does not meet or they meet someone who meet the needs that the kill time relationship does not.

Sex only relationship

Sex only relationships are very common today. Indeed, some marriages can even be described as sex only if they only involve sex. It may seem strange, but a kill time relationship can resemble a sex only relationship if the time spent together only consists of sex. As was touched on previously, love and sex are perceived today as being essential components of a relationship to a relationship that focuses primarily on sex is not perceived as unusual today as it might have been in the past.

Sex only relationships can be dysfunctional, but it has to be recognized that many men and women do have a need for sex and these types of partnerships can meet that need. Issues arise when partners have other needs that are not being met by the sex only relationship. Partners may have a need for intimacy and physical closeness outside of sex, such as kissing or cuddling on the couch, and the sex only relationship would not meet these needs. Also, sex is not the same as love, so the basic need for love would also be absent from this relationship.

Love relationship

The love relationship is considered by some to be the ideal partnership. These partnerships are founded on the purposes of love and feature love as the prevailing element. Of course, what love differs depends on who you ask. For some people, love may be an emotional attachment based on esteem, while for others, love means acceptance. To some people, the most important characteristic is a strong physical attraction (almost an animal magnetism).

Whatever your definition of love is, it is increasingly common for people today to feel that love is an essential characteristic of a relationship. Relationships created because the two partners love each other are regarded as normal today, but they can still come with problems. For example, although love can weather the storm, sometimes it does not. What happens when partners in a love relationship fall out of love? If love is the only thing holding the partnership together, then the bond can break, regardless of how strong the sensation of love once was.

This is sort of the issue that was brought up in the context of discussing marriages in the first chapter. The marriage contract recognized that marriages served several important functions, of which love was regarded as not particularly relevant (if it was present at all). Although most people assume that love relationships are what they should strive for, approaching relationships from the standpoint of needs can help men and women to understand why even these relationships can fail. If you have needs that are not being met by the love relationship, then it should come as no surprise that these partnerships can run into problems.

Sacrificial relationship

Human beings are capable of sacrificing themselves for others. This is a peculiar characteristic that has been observed in other animal species. It is often labeled with the name altruism, which reflects the idea that one person is engaging in an activity that benefits someone else even if it harms the person who does it. A sacrificial relationship is characterized by one partner sacrificing themselves for the other, whether that sacrifice is in the form of time, money, or other relationship commodities that have value.

Although many romantic relationships are notable for sacrifice, the sacrificial relationship is generally used to describe a partnership where the sacrifices are unhealthy because one partner makes sacrifices while the other does not. A sacrificial relationship can, therefore, be a type of selfish or narcissistic relationship in which one person is expected to take on these deprivations for the sake of another. The beneficiary of the sacrifices may perceive themselves as more deserving of resources than the other person. These relationships are therefore notable for a lack of equity or even a lack of respect of one partner for the other.

Love-hate relationship

Love-hate is a term that is frequently tossed around although most people who use it may not fully conceptualize what it means. The love-hate relationship describes a bond in which both parties feel strong feelings of love and hate. They may make loud exclamations of love or hate, or they may engage in activities that make it clear to all that these sorts of feelings are present. One partner may loudly declare that they hate the other and then throw something, while a short time later, they may engage in sexual behavior with one another or other forms of intimacy. There is a histrionic or even borderline quality to these relationships that can make them toxic.

Love-hate relationships are common because of the peculiar nature of attraction. The person we may profess to dislike may be the same one that we are most physically drawn to. There is an Italian movie where an actress pokes fun at her husband's unattractive face yet constantly displays the strong magnetic attraction she has for him. There is a thin line between love and hate, and this represents that human beings are strongly emotional creatures who sometimes act in ways that are nothing short of illogical.

The love-hate relationship is usually problematic. This is because, although love is important for many relationships to endure (romantic or otherwise), most relationships cannot withstand the weight of strong feelings of hate. If one partner in the union truly hates something about the other, then this usually creates a conflict that surfaces in various ways and can only be removed by the termination of the partnership. Ending the partnership can sometimes be difficult because of the great physical attraction that is often present in these relationships, but this can be essential to prevent them from entering into the toxic realm.

We began this chapter by attempting to define what a good relationship is, and the most effective way of addressing that was to talk about what bad ones look like. Good relationships, relationships that serve an important role in your life, are characterized by respect, equity, love, and acceptance. In these sorts of relationships, the human needs for love, affection, safety, and security that are part and parcel of all important human relationships are met. A review of some of the major types of relationships may help the men and women reading to determine if their relationship is a healthier one or perhaps a dysfunctional one.

Putting a label on your relationship is not the end of your foray into understanding your relationship. Indeed, labeling your relationship as this or that can give you a false sense of security by allowing you to believe that your partnership falls into a recognizable pattern. But human relationships can be just as diverse as human beings can be. One person may describe your relationship as a love-hate relationship, while you may see it as merely a playful version of a love relationship in which you take occasional jabs at one another.

What it becomes important for you to do is to then, once you have a basic framework for the type of relationship you have, to then start to analyze what the problems in your relationship are. As we have already seen, even dysfunctional relationships can be salvaged if members are able to invest the time and energy into fixing the problems in the partnership. For example, a common problem in many relationships is communication and addressing these communication issues can be a quick and effective way to nip relationship conflicts in the bud.

Chapter 3: The Importance of Communication

A common complaint in relationships is that there is no communication or that communication is poor. Indeed, after relationship formation communication can suffer as partners may fall into a routine of sorts as they become more used to one another or as passion fails. Communication problems, therefore, can be a natural consequence of relationship progression, or they can be a symptom of a relationship that is failing. As the reader will see at other junctures in this book, asking the question of whether or not a relationship can survive this or that hurdle is an important step in any relationship experiencing problems. Fortunately, for most people hoping to salvage a relationship on the rocks, communication problems can often be resolved with or without the aid of the therapist.

But the first step is to acknowledge that communication is important. Communication is how we generally indicate our wants and needs to those around us. Individuals in romantic relationships have to pay special attention to communication because they often spend prolonged periods with their significant other and may live together. This makes good communication essential in the day to day life of a relationship.

We have all heard the story of the couple that has been married so long that they do not have to communicate and perhaps even sleep in separate beds. This may be taken by some as evidence that communication in a relationship is not as important as some present it to be, but that would be the wrong interpretation. Couples that have been together for a long time and appear to lack communication may actually be so in sync with one another that they communicate in non-verbal ways that others just are not clued into.

Communication Defined

Recognizing the importance of communication, therefore, requires that we first understand what it is. Human beings are not the only animals to be engaged in communicating. Other primates communicate. Other animal's species have ways of communicating with one another. Famously, dolphins have several forms of communication, including sonar and a type of thought projection that some scientists have likened to telepathy.

Taking a quick glance at animal forms of communication reveals that verbal communication, what we typically label in English as "communication," is only one of several ways that human beings have of spreading information to one another. This is precisely what communication is: the various tools that human beings and other organisms use to express thoughts, ideas, or emotions. And communication clearly does not have to involve speech or even language. Apes are able to communicate even though they do not form words or have the ability to write.

In fact, studies of apes have revealed just how important communication is in this animal family. Indeed, communication mechanisms are so consistent among apes that even humans are able to understand what gestures made by other primates mean. An ape may change their body position or lower their head to indicate submission. They may look away when they have a desire not to offend, or they may show their teeth when they want to appease. This showing of the teeth is akin to what we call a smile in humans, although the emotions behind this ape smile are not always the benign sense of happiness or goodwill that we associate with people that do this.

Indeed, studies of apes are revealing that communication in apes can be just as nuanced and false as they can be in human beings. Therefore, the ape smile may not look like a smile to us because the ape is not happy, but scared. This way of using cues like smile and body position to communicate information in ways that are complex and sometimes dishonest helps us to understand the import of human communication. Humans also express information in ways that are not entirely honest, and many of these ways do not involve language at all.

So what are some of the ways that human beings communicate? The following are three important aspects of communication:

- Verbal communication
- Non-verbal communication
- Written language
- Empathy

Verbal communication involves the words that human beings speak to one another. People speak to communicate information of all types and all degrees of importance. Someone may speak to another to communicate their feelings about an incident or they may merely be passing the time by talking about all the action in the recent baseball game. Non-verbal communication consists of the unspoken cues that can convey information, such as body and hand position, facial expression, rapid movements, and distance. Written language is separated from verbal communication because this important category includes written things, such as the modern text which has changed relationships in dramatic ways. We can also say that empathy and emotional intelligence are important forms of communication even though they often rely on the other forms already mentioned.

Communication Problems that Impact Relationships Today

Communication problems form some of the most important causes of relationship conflicts, whether we are highlighting romantic relationships or relationships in general. Problems of communication generally focus on a lack of communication or ineffective communication. This is part of the reason why emotional intelligence focuses on emotional accuracy as an important component. We can say that communication is important to a relationship, but if that communication does not focus on the important things that need to be conveyed, or if the information conveyed is not an accurate representation of what is felt or believed, then this is ineffective communication and a problem in the relationship.

We can divide communication problems into three main areas:

- Lack of communication
- Ineffective communication
- Damaging communication

Lack of communication and ineffective communication has already been explained. Damaging communication is an area that encompasses several behaviors that are characteristic of dysfunctional relationships. Damaging communication can include the harmful and abusive words that the narcissist speaks to their codependent partner. It can also include the false and manipulative words that the manipulator or pathological liar speaks to their target. We can even say that some of the problematic communication of modern technology, like texts or social media, is a form of damaging communication.

There has been much discussion on the potentially damaging effects of information conveyed on social media or via text. Some may ask how this information is any different from a phone call, a letter, or what we described previously as written language, but it must be acknowledged that social media has opened a whole can of worms for relationships, romantic or otherwise. Partners may find themselves stalking their partner on the internet or obsessing about their partner's internet activity. They may become enraged when a partner friend and old flame on social media or may believe a fictitious story that they read on their favorite online platform.

Texts have also become an increasingly popular form of communication both in and out of romantic relationships. Texting is so common that even young children are given cellphones to enable them to communicate with their parents via text. There has not been recognized on a societal level that new forms of communication that stem from technology can be damaging to the individual and cause conflict in a relationship.

Just focusing on relationships, for the time being, texts are replacing face to face contact that partners involved romantically have had since the beginning of the human species. This upfront contact is not only the normal way those primates interact with one another, but it also allows us to gauge the import and honesty of the words that are spoken, and it allows us to form an emotional connection with another person using our emotional intelligence. You cannot have empathy via text, especially as you cannot be entirely sure that the information conveyed is true or not, or what the intentions were when the text was sent.

New forms of communication are distorting the normal ways that human beings interact with one another. It has been argued that communication via text or other online means is part of a society that is becoming more false, narcissistic, and shallow. Although societal issues of technology are outside the scope of this book, it is important to recognize that communication via text or issues of social media can cause problems in a relationship. These problems can be so great that some people decide not to text at all and to disconnect completely via social media. Such people believe that human beings survived for tens of thousands of years without cellphones and the internet, and we can certainly do so today. Whatever you believe, it is important to recognize that not all communication is good communication.

Listening to and Understanding Your Partner

We discuss ways to improve your communication skills in the next chapter, but one of the best things that you can do right now is focused on how well you understand your partner. Partners in a relationship can grow apart. This means that they change over time and no longer understand your partner. Do not assume that your partner is the same person that you began the relationship with. There may be aspects of them that you never saw and understood, sometimes because of your own reasons. Really listening to and forming an emotional connection with your partner is important in understanding them. No matter what stage your relationship is in, this simple step can drastically change the communication dynamic in your relationship.

Chapter 4: 10 Ways to Improve Your Communication Skills

Communication skills are essential in any relationship. Indeed, a lack of communication is one of the major causes of relationship breakdown. What this means for you is that strengthening and maintaining your relationship can be as simple as improving how you communicate with your partner. It is important to recognize that it takes two to tango, and communication problems are generally an issue of both partners rather than just one. Keep that in mind as you put the following communication tips to work in your relationship.

Way Number One. Always be honest in your interactions with your partner.

A good relationship requires that you make an emotional connection with your partner. This can only happen if your partnership is characterized by dishonesty. Dishonesty in a relationship manifests itself in several ways. Your interactions with your partner can feel unsatisfying or stilted. You may find yourself feeling sad and lonely, even though you are in a relationship. When you and your partner commit to always being honest with one another, you protect yourself from a silent killer that can eat away at a relationship.

Way Number Two. Know when your partner may benefit from encouragement and love.

Sometimes we can make a relationship all about us. When we feel strongly about another person, we can see that person as a reflection on ourselves: as sort of a mirror. This is not just true of romantic relationships; it can also be true in a relationship with a parent or child. Therefore, we can sometimes judge the other harshly because we are angry at how their behavior is impacting our own self-image. But sometimes we need to step away from this sort of narcissism and recognize that our partner is an independent human being who needs encouragement and love from us.

Way Number Three. If you notice that you are feeling a certain way emotionally and your partner does not appear receptive, maybe this is a good time to say how you feel.

This is a type of communication that sometimes diminishes as a relationship increases in duration, and that is not a good thing. When people have been together for a long time, they can become comfortable or complacent and not tell their partner when they are feeling sad or emotional because they have gotten used to a sort of emotional distance in a relationship. Emotional connection is important in a long-term romantic relationship (at least the modern relationship that is not entered into for financial reasons). For this reason, not communicating your feelings can gradually eat away at your relationship until neither of you feels anything at all. How can your relationship survive reaching that point? It is better not to let your relationship reach that stage.

Way Number Four. No form of technology (even the phone) can replace face-to-face interaction.

There has not been an appreciation in many sectors of how damaging technology has been to relationships. It was bad enough when people were using telephones as a substitute for face-to-face encounters, but now we have texts and social media. All this does is lead people to feel that they are connected with others, when they actually are not. Interactions made via text or social media are superficial. Real connections are important for you to be satisfied as a human being. Your relationship relies on maintaining real connections.

Way Number Five. Schedule time that you and your partner can discuss your day.

It is easy for partners in a relationship to fall into a routine. This can be all right if you still manage to maintain time where you and your partner have real interactions, but sometimes these interactions fade away. Something that most couples can do to work towards repairing a faltering bond is setting time aside to discuss their day. This allows you to reconnect and rediscover why you fell in love in the first place.

Way Number Six. Know when to disconnect from media (cellphone, social media, and internet).

Because there is no substitute for a good old-fashioned face-to-face, sometimes what is needed is to take technology out of your relationship altogether. When your relationship becomes characterized by social media and texting, then your strong romantic bond will eventually be no different from all those false friendships that you have on social media. You want your relationship to be something different from those, something that will endure. So step away from your phone.

Way Number Seven. Learn how to listen rather than just hear.

Listening actively is important enough that is has been mentioned more than once in this book. It is amazing how bad people can be at listening. Sometimes we have problems with listening because we are so wrapped up in our own concerns that we have difficulty making it less about ourselves and more about others, but it is important to do this. A partner will notice when you do not listen and when you do not seem to care as much about them as you do about yourself. This may be a good time to start listening.

Way Number Eight. Pay attention to the non-verbal cues that indicate how your partner is feeling.

We focus a lot on communication as an important tool in a relationship. It is important to remember that non-verbal communication is just as important in human interactions as verbal communication is. We are primates and we indicate how we feel to others with non-verbal cues just as much as with verbal ones, and in some cases, the non-verbal cues can be more important. Non-verbal cues are particularly important in a relationship because they lead to an emotional connection so pay attention to them.

Way Number Nine. Not everyone is a talker, and that's okay, but when in doubt, communicates.

We talked about communication in the context of expressing your emotions, but communication is important in all aspects of your thoughts (and expressing them). Although some people may be reserved, quiet, or just don't have much to say, as humans we are wired to communicate, so it is important to be attuned to situations where your partner needs you to express yourself.

Way Number Ten. If all else fails, consider seeing a therapist help with your communication woes.

Most relationship problems can be resolved if partners in a relationship are committed to working towards fixing them. Some people give up on relationships or subconsciously want the relationship to fail, but if you are reading this because it is probably because you want to improve your relationship. Although there is much that you can do, sometimes it is not enough. When all else fails, you should be open to obtaining help from a therapist.

Chapter 5: Emotional Intelligence

Emotional intelligence emerged from a period where many had grown frustrated with more traditional models of intelligence. These models perceived intelligence is being merely a function of cognitive ability. The measured intelligence with IQ tests, which are often used to make educational decisions for children, such as whether a child should be put in a remedial or special class, or to make predictions about the sort of success (or lack thereof) that a child might expect in the future. It became obvious to social scientists in the 1960s and 1970s that there was more to human ability than merely the ability to solve problems. This is how the world of emotional intelligence came into being.

Of course, the first question is why should anyone be talking about emotional intelligence in the context of relationships? We have seen that relationships are characterized by love, respect, esteem, and acceptance. Relationships of a romantic nature meet the basic needs that human beings have, in addition to physical needs for sex in many cases. Except for love, none of the needs on Maslow's hierarchy of needs addresses emotion. If a relationship has love, is it important for partners to think about how they relate to one another emotionally?

The answer, of course, is yes. One only needs to think about what love is in order to understand the role that emotional intelligence plays in a relationship. Love is a feeling characterized by caring for another deeply, and this comes with other qualities like respect and acceptance. One cannot really love another if one is unable to understand them or connect with them on an emotional level. Emotional intelligence is a spectrum of skills that allow human beings to connect emotionally.

In fact, emotional intelligence can be overlooked in relationships because it is not well understood by many. Some people see excessive emotionality as a problem in a relationship. Those who see emotions this way are likely to hear the term emotional intelligence and think of a sort of quack subject that came out of the hippie period of the 60s. Although there is some truth in the assertion that emotional intelligence emerged from a time where people were addressing things that they thought they understood with different spectacles (like intelligence), research on the subject has revealed that emotional intelligence skills are important in successful careers, successful lives, and successful relationships.

Emotional intelligence is not the same as emotionality. So-called emotional people are said to be constantly under the influence of their feelings, using them to guide their behaviors, often without regard for the feelings that others have. Emotional people are viewed as being impulsive or even unstable, which is perceived as being a potential stressor or source of conflict in a relationship. Although it is true that people like this can be problematic in relationships, the label of emotional here is perhaps an unfair one. People like this should be properly described as histrionic, or perhaps another personality disorder label can be found (if a label is needed at all).

Emotion and emotionality are terms that sometimes have negative connotations, and the emotional intelligence discussion seeks to rectify that. Emotional intelligence is critical to relationships because people who lack this type of intelligence will have difficulty connecting with others deeply, and this includes having deep personal relationships. Human beings use emotional intelligence skills to understand and relate to one another, even if they do not realize they are doing this or have never heard of emotional intelligence.

Emotional intelligence allows men and women to be smart about how they interact with others, using a type of innate intelligence that they have. And that is precisely what emotional intelligence is. It is one of several types of intelligence that human beings can display, representing an essential aspect of our human nature. Although attention has always been given in science to cognitive and spatial abilities as encapsulated in IQ testing, emotional intelligence is being shown to not only be just as important as intelligence measured by IQ tests but perhaps more important.

The importance of emotional intelligence has led to the development of several different tests that seek to measure this essential human skill. Emotional intelligence also called emotional quotient (or EQ), is something that is being actively studied as an important quality in leaders. The emphasis on emotional intelligence has naturally led to a shift away from IQ as a measure that is given great importance in schools as a predictor of ability and success.

Emotional intelligence is the range of capabilities that allow human beings to form connections with one another emotionally. Although different models of emotional intelligence define this quantity in alternate ways, perhaps the most enduring one sees emotional intelligence as involving five essential skills. Just as with cognitive ability, the individual skills in emotional intelligence work together to allow men and women to behave with emotional smart.

What Is Emotional Intelligence?

The skills that together comprise emotional intelligence include emotional awareness, emotional self-regulation, motivation, empathy, and using emotions as a guide for action. As we will see later in this chapter, all of these must be used together even if each individual quality has its value. For example, being able to determine your own emotions and the emotions of others accurately (emotional awareness) is important on its own, although it needs to be used together with self-regulation for one to be truly emotionally intelligent.

Self-regulation in emotional intelligence refers to the ability to halt or alter one's own emotions. It is necessary to do this because our emotions can be dysfunctional at times. Although anger or agitation can be legitimate feelings that we have in particular situations, it may be important for functional reasons to limit these. It will be difficult to work successfully at a job if one is constantly giving in to feelings of anger or rage. One must frequently limit these feelings. This is also true in a relationship.

Empathy is a quality that is often used as a stand-in for emotional intelligence, even though it has its own separate meaning. Empathy refers to the ability to share the emotions and experiences of another person.

Empathy can also be mistaken for sympathy. There are alternative definitions of empathy, but most see sympathy as being an important part of empathy. Sympathy is the ability to feel compassion and tolerance for another person, and it is not hard to see why sympathy would be important in empathy. But feeling compassion for someone is not the same as sharing the same emotional state as someone else, which is what empathy represents.

Perhaps the last important component of emotional intelligence is the ability to use emotions as a guide for your behavior. Although this may engender visions of the histrionic person basing all of their behaviors on emotions, this is not what this phrase refers to. Once one is emotionally aware and able to regulate one's own dysfunctional emotions, one can then have empathy for others and be motivated to act based on these deep emotional sensitivities. The idea here is that your emotional sensitivities allow you to behave in a way more beneficial to you and others.

How to Feel and Handle Your Emotions

Emotional intelligence has little value if people do not take steps to hone their emotional intelligence skills. Being emotionally intelligent can change your relationship in dramatic ways. Indeed, emotional intelligence can save a relationship. Because we live in a society where men and women are disconnected from one another in various ways, despite all of the electronic ways we have of communicating, emotional intelligence allows us to connect with each other in a deeply human way. Some have even argued that we live in a traumatized society: traumatized by things we hear on the news and social media. Emotional intelligence allows us to return to our humanness and heal from trauma, including relationship trauma. Here we will review some of the emotional intelligence facts that can help you feel and handle your emotions better in a relationship. These facts are listed below:

- Empathy is a critical part of being emotionally intelligent.
- Research suggests that empathy is not only important in relationships but in leadership.
- Emotional intelligence is a skill that can be acquired.
- Emotional intelligence is a type of intelligence similar to cognitive ability or spatial reasoning.
- Individuals with emotional intelligence are able to use this skill in all of their relationships, not just romantic ones.
- Having sympathy and having empathy is not the same thing.
- Emotional intelligence does not involve using just one ability, but several that work in tandem.
- Individuals who lack self-regulation do not truly demonstrate emotional intelligence.
- Non-verbal communication is an essential component of emotional intelligence as it allows us to be cued in to the emotions of others.
- Active listening is an important part of empathy as well as emotional intelligence in general.

Fact One. Empathy is a critical part of being emotionally intelligent.

Empathy is so important to emotional intelligence that some early writers on the subject focused solely on empathy as an indication of emotional intellectual capacity. Empathy is important to emotional intelligence because it represents an innate ability that human beings have to form a connection without words. Communication is often cited as an important determinant of the success or failure of a relationship, but because human beings are able to connect without the need for words having empathy can be just as important as communication.

Empathy is the ability to share the subjective feelings and experiences of another. Although this does appear to be a uniquely human capability, there is evidence that empathy or something like it may exist in other animals, including other primates: our closest relatives. Although all aspects of emotional intelligence should lead to an emotional connection formed between two people, empathy represents emotional intelligence in miniature. The capacity to be emotionally aware and to form a connection because it can occur all in one step with empathy.

Fact Two. Research suggests that empathy is not only important in relationships but in leadership.

Much of the research on empathy focuses on the role that empathy plays for leaders. This is in part because workers often report that their managers lack empathy and they note that it is a major source of dissatisfaction. But it is also true that businesses recognize that managers with better leadership skills can get more out of their workers, so they have led the charge in training their leaders on empathy. This research is important as the role that empathy plays in business is not as obvious as it is in romantic relationships.

Research has found that leaders with empathy are rated more highly by their staff and are regarded as better at their jobs than those without empathy. It has also been shown that although empathy is important in all leadership settings, this quality appears to be more important in some cultures than in others. For example, research suggests that in cultures where there is more economic and social distance between managers and staff, empathy is rated as being more important among the management.

Fact Three. Emotional intelligence is a skill that can be acquired.

One of the most important aspects of emotional intelligence is that, although emotional intelligence skills can be native in many people, EI skills can be acquired by those who are willing to work at it. This is an aspect that is particularly important to partners in relationships because it indicates that a partner who looks EI (or EQ) is not necessarily hopeless. With the right sort of exercises, emotional intelligence skills can be improved, leading to dramatic changes in relationships.

One of the best ways that emotional intelligence skills can be improved is by practicing empathy. This may sound strange, but it essentially means that the individual practices having concern for others and showing this concern. This generally means asking how others are doing and genuinely caring about the answers that they give you. Research suggests that those who practice empathy in this manner eventually come to show empathy spontaneously.

Honing EI skills do not only apply to empathy. Another important component of emotional intelligence that should be practiced (and which many people lack) is self-regulation. Self-regulation refers to the ability of accurately recognizing when one's emotional state is dysfunctional and making an effort to change or stop those feelings. As this is a skill that many partners in relationships lack, practicing self-regulation in the form of saying to oneself things like "This anger is problematic, I need to change it," can lead to this sort of step becoming unconscious over time.

Fact Four. Emotional intelligence is a type of intelligence similar to cognitive ability or spatial reasoning.

Although we do not go into detail on the history of the study of emotional intelligence in this book, this quality emerged from a time when there was somewhat of an obsession with intelligence quotient (IQ) in the scientific community. IQ tests were being given to children in schools, mental patients, and workers at their place of employment. In particular, IQ tests in schools were being used to make important educational decisions about children.

Many parents were concerned that IQ tests were not accurately measuring the abilities of their children. Aside from whether IQ tests measure cognitive ability well, there was a belief that there were other types of intelligence that were not being addressed by IQ at all. Indeed, some at this early stage was making the important observation that success in life was not always tied to intelligence, but other factors seemed to be at play. Emotional intelligence, therefore, emerged after thirty years of study.

Today, EI is regarded as equivalent to other forms of intelligence, like cognitive ability. Indeed, emotional intelligence is regarded as of such importance that research is being done to figure out how artificial intelligence can be programmed to display this type of intelligence. The idea is that machines with artificial intelligence should be able to interact with humans the way that people interact with one another, which requires that these artificial intelligence agents be sensitive to things like nuanced expressions of emotion and be able to respond in ways that demonstrate sympathy.

Fact Five. Individuals with emotional intelligence can use this skill in all of their relationships, not just romantic ones.

One of the more important aspects of emotional intelligence, especially as regards relationships, is that individuals use this skill in all of their interactions with other people. Emotional intelligence is not something that we turn on and off, but it permeates the way that we interact with others: guiding us to behave with awareness, compassion, and understanding. Emotional intelligence also allows people to be in sync in ways that are difficult to accomplish with mere words.

A famous singer once said that words were useless, and this seems to be a subliminal message in emotional intelligence. Of course, we use words to alert others of how we feel, but we can accomplish this task without words. Indeed, emotional intelligence represents the capacity of human beings that lies below the surface. It involves ways that human beings have of interacting and connecting based on pure emotional awareness and emotional understanding. These sorts of emotional skills will be present in all relationships that the emotionally intelligent person has, not just the romantic ones.

Fact Six. Having sympathy and having empathy is not the same thing.

Empathy is a concept that is not well understood by many people. For this reason, the words sympathy and empathy are often used interchangeably even though they are both important. Indeed, many definitions of empathy include sympathy within the definition. So the ability to feel compassion and tolerance for others (sympathy) is part of sharing the subjective emotions and experiences of others, which is empathy.

Although it may seem pedantic to focus on this distinction, it is important in the context of close relationships, especially romantic ones. An emotionally intelligent romantic partner should not only have sympathy for their significant other, but they should actually come to share the feelings of the other, rather than merely understand them. This sharing of emotions represents the close, unspoken emotional connection which represents that the romantic partners are not friends or acquaintances but involved in an enduring relationship. A partner who is emotionally intelligent will be able to sense when their significant other has sympathy, but not empathy and this can create a barrier that can eventually lead to conflict.

Fact Seven. Emotional intelligence does not involve using just one ability, but several that work in tandem.

One of the fascinating things about emotional intelligence is that the abilities that comprise it are all used together, even though they have separate value. Therefore empathy is used together with awareness, self-regulation, and actions motivated by emotion to create a person who behaves with particularly human sensitivity. This means that being good in one area is not enough to make someone emotional intelligent. Indeed, lacking one or more of the other areas can actually cause someone to behave in a very problematic way emotionally.

Fact Eight. Individuals who lack self-regulation do not truly demonstrate emotional intelligence.

Therefore, a person who is strong in one area of emotional intelligence can lack overall emotional intelligence because they are deficient in one of the EI areas that are essential for the whole machine to operate. This is particularly the case for self-regulation: the ability to alter one's emotional state. Self-regulation is used along with emotional awareness to create someone who is sensitive emotionally, but who recognizes when their emotions (and the actions that stem from them) may be a problem.

For example, if you are aware of your emotions and act on them anyway (regardless of their nature), then you are not very different from a histrionic or borderline person who is constantly displaying strong feelings of love, hate, or lust because that is what you happen to be feeling at the moment. Self-regulation means that you are able to determine the appropriateness of your emotions, which is essential in behaving in a way that is not only sensitive for you but for others.

Fact Nine. Non-verbal communication is an essential component of emotional intelligence as it allows us to be cued into the emotions of others.

Non-verbal communication is a critical component of emotional intelligence. This should come as no surprise as emotional intelligence involves the many cues that we use to gauge the emotional state of others and behave accordingly. Not all of the cues that alert us to the feelings of others are verbal. The facial expression, body position, or even distance can be clues as to how the other is feeling. These important clues permeate all aspects of emotional intelligence, including empathy and emotional awareness. Paying more attention to the non-verbal cues of your partner can help you to become more emotionally intelligent.

Fact Ten. Active listening is an important part of empathy as well as emotional intelligence in general.

Much of this chapter on emotional intelligence has focused on abstractions like awareness and empathy that some may find difficult to adapt to their lives right away. We have seen that these are important in helping you to have a relationship infused with all of the benefits of emotional intelligence, but that does not make it easy. Active listening is something that you can do to set yourself on the way to being more emotionally intelligent. Active listening means not only hearing what someone is saying but paying attention to the words, understanding them and their import. Non-verbal communication may be important to emotional intelligence, but that does not mean we can ignore basic communication skills. Especially if one or more partners lack in EI, an act as simple as being better at active listening can make a big difference.

Chapter 6: Understanding and Overcoming Your Fears

Fear exists for an important reason. It is easy to think of fear as something that is always dysfunctional, as in post-traumatic stress disorder (or PTSD), where a heightened fear response triggered by ordinary things can prevent a man or woman from living a healthy, happy life. But conditions like PTSD represent a natural response gone awry. The problem is not fear itself. The problem is allowing fear to dictate your life.

For example, most people are afraid of snakes. We should be afraid of snakes because snakes are generally dangerous to humans. Sure, there are men and women who keep snakes as pets and are able to have a pretty safe relationship with their essentially dangerous pets, but it would be silly to think that just because we know someone who has a pet snake that we should feel no fear when we hear a rattlesnake or see a spitting cobra. We are afraid of snakes for a reason: because our brain is wired to recognize and remember danger. We are especially sensitive to danger because we evolved to be this way. If we were not afraid of scary things then we would have likely gone extinct as a species tens of thousands of years ago.

Fear really becomes a problem in two situations. The first situation we mentioned in passing. Fear that we allow to take over our lives clearly becomes a problem. In this situation, our fear is not illegitimate, but we allow it to dictate the daily experience and course of our life. This is essentially the case in people with PTSD. It would be incorrect to say that their fears of loud noises or crowds are not legitimate, but they also need to learn to manage their fears in order to live a normal life.

The other situation in which fear becomes a problem is when we feel fear in situations in which we should not feel fear. This is the case in traumatized persons. Women and men who have been traumatized because of abuse in childhood or even in adulthood can be very sensitive to places and people that remind them of their abuse. It may even be true that such people fear everyone and most situations because they never had people in their lives they were able to trust.

Where Fear Comes From in Relationships

It is interesting to examine where these sorts of fears originate in relationships. Think about it. Some individuals are very easy going when it comes to their relationship. If their partner is going alone to a setting where there may be many attractive people of the opposite sex, this may not bother them. This is because they feel secure enough in their own skin and in their relationship that they do not feel fear at the prospect of their partner cheating on them or hurting them emotionally.

This really gets at where fear comes from in a relationship. Fears about things that most people generally do not feel fear from indicating a sense of insecurity. And here we do not mean insecurity as a personal failing, which is sometimes implied in the usage of the term. We mean insecurity that stems from problematic attachment patterns that develop during childhood. Children who have caregivers who did not respond adequately to their needs develop what is called an insecure attachment. Essentially this means that they are not put at ease by the presence of their caregiver, and they regard the world with a level of danger or hostility that is atypical and dysfunctional.

This pattern of insecure attachment in childhood persists in later life and can become an obsessive fear in the context of a relationship. A person may feel fear of abandonment; they may feel constant jealousy. Although some of these types of fears can be felt by those with more typical development patterns, they are associated with people who had the sort of insecure attachment to their caregivers that we just described. Whatever the ultimate source of fear in your relationship is, there are steps that you can take to work on your fears and overcome them as part of your general goal of relationship improvement.

Overcome Your Fears by Talking

One of the most powerful ways that you can overcome your fears of abandonment and jealousy in a relationship is by talking. This tactic really hits at the source of fear in most people. The source of fear is an inaccurate assessment of the situation or interpretation of events. In other words, you perceive danger when there really is not any danger. This is not too different from the PTSD person who hears a loud noise and thinks a bomb is going off, or the anxious person who thinks that every person they meet will dislike them because there is something fundamentally dislikable about themselves.

The biggest step that you can take to overcome this sort of fear is to create an accurate picture rather than an accurate one. In a serious romantic relationship, communication is often the best way to do this. If you hear that your partner is going out and you are afraid that they might meet someone better than you and might leave you, communicating with your partner by saying things like "I am a little scared about all the attractive women you might meet at the bar, but I trust you": this can stimulate a conversation that not only will allay your fears, but allow your partner to understand where you are coming from.

What happens when you do not talk about your fears with your partner is that your partner then jumps to his or her own conclusions about what is going on with you. So your partner may think that you do not want him or her to go to the work gathering because you are manipulative and controlling when it is really because you are scared. Talking, therefore not only helps you to overcome your fears, but it helps to improve your relationship by stimulating a better understanding between you and your partner.

Chapter 7: Couple Conflicts

Conflict will naturally arise in any relationship, romantic or otherwise. The only relationships in which conflicts do not arise are those in which the interests and motivations of both partners are so closely aligned that there is no impetus for conflict because the twain sees everything the same way. This sort of situation is rare. You see this in the friend relationship, in which people were friends first and know one another extremely well. You also see this in twins, people who are in a manner of speaking copies of one another and therefore are unlikely to experience conflicts because of deep similarity.

But most relationships experience a conflict of some sort or another. This conflict does not have to be physical or emotional. Oftentimes, this conflict takes the appearance of disagreements over little things that spiral out of control because of how partners mismanage conflict. Indeed, in this regard, conflicts in relationships resemble fear in relationships because it stems from an inability to manage something that naturally arises.

Some people believe that the solution to couple conflicts is not to have conflict at all, and this is problematic thinking. This wish becomes problematic because the usual way two people that are different become aligned to the extent that they no longer experience conflict is by one person choosing (or being coerced into) following the lead or giving in to the desires of the other person. This sort of dynamic smacks of narcissism, as one person chooses to place their own wants and needs above those of another, and this is the epitome of a dysfunctional relationship.

So once we have established that it is normal for relationships to have conflict, and we have determined that the problem really is how people deal with that conflict, now we can start to think of what some common reasons for conflict in a relationship are. In reality, there are so many things that can cause couples to disagree that it becomes impossible to list them all, but the following are some examples that may resonate with readers:

- The goals of the partners in a relationship do not align (e.g., life goals)
- The partners have different personality traits that make it hard for them to get along
- The needs of one or both partners in the relationship are not being met
- The partners entered the relationship for the wrong reasons
- One partner feels mistreated or neglected by the other partner
- The partners are not right for one another, which can lead to one member of the relationship feeling jealous or anxious
- One partner is unable to accept the other and has a desire to change them
- Partners fall out of love with one another and this manifests in a conflict of various kinds

A relationship can have conflicts originating from one or more of these general reasons. For example, one partner who is very different from their other half may feel a desire to change them into the partner they want to be. This can lead to arguments and emotional abuse due to the frustration that one partner has that the other will not change, and the hurt the other feels at being regarded as less than their partner and not being accepted for who they are.

Although some relationship problems are too great to be overcome, many problems that couples have can be mollified. In fact, we can say that the first step in remedying the situation is being honest about what the problems are and taking the necessary steps to change them. In the next chapter, we will examine how these difficulties in a relationship can be fixed with a little bit of elbow grease.

Chapter 8: Overcoming Relationship Difficulties

The problems in your relationship do not have to be an impediment to you and your partner achieving the relationship that you want and deserve. There are changes that the two of you can make in the way that you interact with one another or behave in general that can drastically alter the trajectory of your relationship. It is important to note here that this is not about changing your partner. If your partner still loves to spend $500 a month on comic books or spend Friday nights playing the slot machines, the focus here is not on changing those sorts of behaviors. The point here is to focus on those relationship behaviors that lead to conflict and poor communication.

It may seem to some as if communication is a common theme here and it is. A serious relationship cannot exist if there is not positive communication of some kind. Even eye contact in the form of a kind or loving look is a type of communication that can be necessary for a relationship. Indeed, partners who have been together for many years and have fallen out of love often avoid looking at one another as well as other indications of intimacy because their relationship has frankly lost that intimacy.

Here we focus on some ways that you can overcome relationship difficulties. As we have seen, no serious, long-term relationship is free of problems. If your relationship has no problems you are either involved with your twin or in a bromance. Many relationship problems require a specific fix to resolve them. For example, if the long-term goals of you and your partner are not aligned, then the solution of your difficulty is to come up with a shared goal so you can occupy common ground. If the problem in the relationship is that one person's needs are not being met, then the solution may be that the other partner should find a way to work towards meeting those needs.

Specific problems in a relationship often require specific solutions, but there are general things that partners can do in a relationship to steer the boat on a more positive course. These are general tips that you can incorporate along with other skills and tips that have been mentioned elsewhere.

- Being better about managing common spaces and times
- Learning to share new experiences
- Extending your interests

These suggestions represent ways that you can compromise with your partner. Although human beings are creatures of habit and we have our ways of doing things that make us comfortable, sometimes making a little modification here and there can be beneficial in a relationship. These general sorts of tweaks can help you overcome such problems as differences in goals, inability to accept one another, and even a diminishing of love in the relationship.

Managing common spaces and times allows you to reduce conflicts that arise from resource allocation in the relationship, such as who gets which car on weekends, which controls the remote, who decides where to go out on free times. By managing these things better, a partner who feels that they are overlooked can feel as if they are more of an equal, as they should be. Sharing new experiences with your partner can help you remember why you fell in love with them in the first place. Broadening your interests also can aid you in coming up with common goals that help keep the relationship healthy.

Chapter 9: 10 Secrets to Improving Your Relationship

Fortunately, for many people seeking to improve their relationships, there are some quick tools at hand to help accomplish this. Although most relationship problems are longstanding and cannot be fixed overnight, some steps can be absorbed and taken to hasten the progress that can be made in a relationship. In this chapter, we review some of the secrets that any person interested in moving their relationship in the right direction can take.

Secret One. Be motivated to work on your relationship.

Motivation is something that men and women frequently take for granted. Just as no one should expect to become an Olympic-quality skier without being motivated to put in the work, one also cannot be expected to make the necessary changes in their relationship without being motivated to do so. Being motivated means that you are not passively watching as you and your partner engage in the same old behaviors that caused your relationship to deteriorate over the years that you were together. Indeed, this type of approach is lethargy and the opposite of motivation in this context.

Motivation means that you acknowledge that your relationship has problems and that you may be part of the problem. Being motivated means that you have a desire to change your relationship, taking the necessary steps in order to do so. This involves figuring out what the problem areas are and putting one foot in front of the other every day to fix them.

Secret Two. Have empathy for your partner.

This is something that everyone in a relationship should do, but many are not the best at. A relationship cannot thrive if it is based on negative emotions like hatred, disgust, or loathing. For you to have a successful romantic relationship with your partner, you need to be able to connect with your partner in such a way that you share (and remember) the positive feelings that brought you together in the first place. These are feelings of love, acceptance, and shared interests that naturally exist in people who are meant for one another.

Empathy is how the positive vibes in your emotion can be shared. Empathy means experiencing the subjective feelings and experiences of your partner, and sometimes, these are negative. But the act of sharing these feelings, an act motivated by love and consideration, is in and of itself a positive act. This is the true power of empathy, and this is why empathy is so important in emotional intelligence.

Secret Three. Give your partner their own personal space.

People need personal space today as much as they ever have before. The world seems to be more crowded than ever, and this may in part be due to technology that makes us connected constantly in ways that we were not in the past. Indeed, it seems as if people today constantly have to deal with the intrusion of others, even if part of that is our fault. We set up social media accounts and place our private information there, creating a world where privacy is more difficult to obtain.

But what this means is that personal space is at a premium and it's particularly important. Just as you need your own alone time to process your feelings and the events of the day, your partner needs this two because they are a human dealing with significant experiences just like you are. Although it may seem strange to give someone space in the context of a relationship that appears to be floundering, this space can help both you and your partner work on yourselves so that you can be a better you in the relationship.

Secret Four. Understand that both partners have needs in the relationship.

A concept that we have tried to stress in this book is the importance of understanding needs in a relationship. Just as human beings have needs as individuals, men and women in relationships also have needs. Sometimes, the easiest way to figure out why a relationship is failing is to think about whose needs are not being met. People often think of sexual needs when they think about this sort of deficit in a relationship, but sometimes partners have sufficient physical intimacy, but there is a need for an emotional connection that the sex act is not meeting.

By thinking about your needs and your partner's needs, you can set yourself on the road to an improved relationship. Sometimes, partners in a relationship can be so focused on what they need that they completely ignore what the other partner needs. Perhaps you need to have a vibrant sex life in the relationship, but your partner has needs that are more along the lines of an intimate dinner, a kiss, or a show of affection. If the needs of both partners are not addressed, then an important underlying problem in the relationship will always remain.

Secret Five. Recognize that in the most successful relationships, both partners see themselves as members of a team.

There is no such thing as the perfect relationship, but there are certainly partnerships that are better than others. As we have seen in our discussion of the love-hate relationship (and other dysfunctional relationship types), relationships were the partners have an adversarial relationship usually run into problems. These types of relationships often fail. Physical intimacy that characterizes many relationships today often is not enough to save a relationship where the partners are at odds with each other.

This state of being at odds does not have to stem from a love-hate type of relationship. Your relationship may be filled with love and esteem, but perhaps you do not see eye to eye on certain things. You want to live in the city, and your partner wants to live in the country. You dream of an expensive Architectural Digest type of apartment in New York, and your partner wants to sell everything and travel the world. Opposites may attract, and it is certainly okay for partners in a relationship to have their differences, but if you are unwilling to work together towards a common goal then your relationship has a pretty big stumbling block. Try to find these common goals and work as a team to accomplish them.

Secret Six. Love your partner, but understand that love is not always enough.

Love is the one word that everyone associates with marriage and other serious long-term relationships. This was not always the case. Until recently, some might have said that financial security and common goals in terms of finances was the most important feature of a relationship. Indeed, financial problems in a relationship can form a major source of tension that can derail the partnership. Of course, the point is that our modern idea of relationships seems to ignore that as important as love is, love is not always enough.

This is not to say that love cannot hold a relationship together in spite of everything else that might tear it asunder. Love certainly can be the glue that keeps a couple bonded, but it must be acknowledged that things change in a relationship. People fall out of love. Sometimes the nature of the love that is felt changes, from physical attraction to esteem and admiration. If you want to improve your relationship, you should not use love as a crutch that leads you to ignore problems in the partnership that need work. If you want to make things better, you will have to work towards making the right sorts of changes, love or not.

Secret Seven. Sometimes what's missing in a relationship is active listening.

Listening is one of those things that people think they do but often do not. Hearing someone is not the same as listening to them. Your partner may tell you that their boss at work did this or that, but perhaps what they are really saying is that they are hurt by something their boss said and they need you to give them a little confidence boost. Perhaps they need a sign of affection from you. Hearing the facts of the conversation are not enough here. Listening means reading between the lines and getting a sense of what is not being said.

This is not as difficult as it seems. Two people who are involved in a serious relationship should be connected enough that they can pick up on the little cues that indicate emotional state. Your partner does not have to tell you: "I am angry." If you are listening actively, you should be able to figure out that they are angry. Active listening is a very simple tool that can work wonders in any relationship.

Secret Eight. Recognize that people change. You are just as likely to change over time as your partner is.

One of the hardest things for people in a relationship to recognize is that people change. Even parents sometimes have a hard time recognizing that their children have changed and are not the mischievous little mites that they used to be. In just the same way your partner may change: change interests, change desires, even change their life goals. If you want to keep your relationship strong, you need to recognize that change is natural. We all change as we age and mature, and accepting this evolution can be the key to improving your relationship.

Secret Nine. Don't be a narcissist.

Narcissism involves a set of personality traits and behaviors that can be extremely damaging to a relationship. Narcissists not only put themselves first, they believe that they are imbued with a special quality that makes their needs more important than others. They behave with wanton disregard for others, sometimes even doing things to harm them. The narcissist does this both consciously and subconsciously as they need to uplift their own self-image, which can require that they tear others down. Although most people do not have a narcissistic personality disorder, we all can have narcissistic traits. Don't be a narcissist. Regard your partner's needs and happiness as just as important as your own.

Secret Ten. Learn to accept your partner.

Learning to accept your partner can be easier said than done. Sometimes we see the person we are with as a reflection on ourselves so we can be motivated to change them in order to make them align with our own self-image. But your partner is an independent being who has a right to decide who they want to be and why. Although your intentions in trying to change your partner may be good, this attempt at change can be a serious stressor on your partner and, frankly, it isn't fair to them. If you truly love your partner and are committed to preserving the relationship, then you must learn to accept them for who they are.

Chapter 10: Survey: What Kind of Couple Are You?

Although no two relationships are the same, there are patterns in partnerships that can help men and women see what sort of problems exist in their relationship. In this chapter, we help you identify what kind of couple you and your partner are so that you can think about what the underlying problems in your relationship may be. We do this in the form of a survey. Answering these questions with honesty and accuracy is important to avoid the urge to sugarcoat or to exaggerate your good qualities and diminish the negative ones.

Tip to complete the quiz: Record how many points you received with each question and total them at the end to see what kind of couple you are.

1. We have been together for:

a. A few days

b. A few months

c. Over a year

d. About a year

a = 10 points

b = 40 points

c = 30 points

d = 20 points

2. The Valentine's Day gift that I would most like to receive is:

a. Jewelry

b. Flowers

c. Nothing.

d. A gift card to buy something at the store I like best

a = 20 points

b = 30 points

c = 40 points

d = 10 points

3. We met:

a. Through mutual friends

b. At a club

c. On an online dating website

d. At school or work

a = 10 points

b = 20 points

c = 30 points

d = 40 points

4. My idea of the ideal spot for a date is:

a. An expensive restaurant

b. A hip bar in town

c. The beach

d. A reading or open mic at the bookstore

a = 40 points

b = 20 points

c = 30 points

d = 10 points

5. Throughout the course of the day, I text:

a. Hardly at all because I'm too busy

b. Pretty much all day

c. Once or twice

d. Not at all

a = 20 points

b = 40 points

c = 30 points

d = 10 points

6. The part of my partner's body I am most drawn to is their:

a. Enchanting Eyes

b. Soft lips

c. Arms

d. Hair

a = 30 points

b = 40 points

c = 20 points

d = 10 points

7. If I had to pick a movie to watch with my partner, I would choose

a. The Notebook

b. Austin Powers

c. Philadelphia

d. Die Another Day

a = 40 points

b = 20 points

c = 30 points

d = 10 points

8. For fun, my partner and I like to:

A. Relax together at home

b. Hang out with friends or family

c. Break out Scrabble or Monopoly

d. Take a trip to the theater for a movie

a = 10 points

b = 30 points

c = 20 points

d = 40 points

9. I would describe my relationship as:

a. Physical

b. Basically a bromance

c. Spicy

d. Nice and relaxing

a = 30 points

b = 10 points

c = 40 points

d = 20 points

10. I usually settle disagreements with my partner by:

a. Avoiding talking to them for several days

b. Shouting and getting physical

c. Trying to find common ground

d. We rarely disagree

a = 30 points

b = 20 points

c = 10 points

d = 40 points

This is the time to total your points. Are you ready? Here is where your relationship falls.

100-160 points: Love relationship or Friendly couple

The two of you are so relaxed around one another that people often mistake you for friends. This may be because you started out as friends, have been together for a long time, or just vibe together in a natural way.

170-250 points: Love-hate relationship

Your relationship can be so volatile that others often wonder why you don't just call it quits. In spite of this, you know why you are still together.

260-320 points: Equally-matched or Twin couple

The two of you are so similar that you might as well be twins. A better way to describe might be to call you equally-matched.

330-400 points: Power couple

You may have your differences, but you get on well together and are drama free. You are the power couple: the partnership that many others aspire to be.

Frequently Asked Questions

1. Why is learning about relationships important?
   Most people taking the step of learning about relationships do so because they are interested in "fixing" their relationship or, at the very least, identifying why their relationship may be experiencing problems. Learning about relationships allows people to improve the relationships they have and to form new ones with insight. Another aspect of this issue is that men and women often form relationships for the wrong reasons, and when these relationships fail, they do not understand why. Although it is not for anyone to judge the reasons why two individuals choose to form a partnership, identifying what the components of a good relationship are and what such a relationship looks like can help understand why some relationships do not work out in the end. This can also help you ensure that you do not make the same mistakes twice.

2. What role do relationships play among humans?
   Human beings are social animals. This means that relationships play an essential and important role in human life on earth. Human beings, just like other primates, naturally form bonds of one kind or another with other human beings. This allows us to

relate to one another in safe, normal, and appropriate ways, and to understand our own place in the larger social grouping.

At the most basic level, relationships exist because they helped to enhance human chances of survival. If relationship formation did not serve a basic, fundamental benefit, then this type of social unit would not have evolved. Romantic relationships, friendships, familial bonds: all of these serve an essential function in the human journey. Beyond basic needs for procreation and species survival, relationships also allow us to meet our needs as individuals.

3. Are relationships essential to humans or can men and women get by without them?

All of the evidence suggests that human beings need relationships to be happy and functional within the human social group. Some may take issue with this assertion. They might argue that, well, I prefer to be on my own or people get on my nerves and I do better when I can do my own thing without having to deal with others. Although different personality types mean that some people may be more individualistic or reserved, which is perfectly all right, success in life generally requires maintaining relationships of some kind.

For example, you have to have a good working relationship with your employer if you want to keep your job. It is a good idea to have a good relationship with your doctor, therapist, or an attorney since you rely on their goodwill to get the things you need. Therefore, though one might say that a romantic or close personal relationship may not be essential, it would be quite a stretch to say that men and women can get by with no relationships at all. It is easy to take for granted that many of the interactions we have to involve a relationship of some kind.

4. Should romantic relationships be approached differently from other types of relationships?

    Romantic relationships are different from other relationships in important ways. For example, a romantic relationship typically has a physical aspect that is often absent from other types of relationships. But when it comes to the basic components of the relationship, these are generally consistent, whether or not the relationship is physical. For example, partners have a need to be loved and accepted. They need to feel safe and secure in the relationship. They have a basic need for financial security, et cetera.

Therefore a romantic relationship can be approached from the same standpoint as any other relationship. You can ask the questions: what are my needs in this relationship and are my needs being met? If the answer is no, then this may be a problem.

5. What is emotional intelligence?

   Emotional intelligence refers to a range of capabilities that have received increased attention. According to the multiple intelligences model, human beings possess many different types of intelligence. Cognitive ability is the traditional type of intelligence, while others such as social intelligence and emotional intelligence have been suggested as other types. Emotional intelligence is important because some research suggests that this type of intelligence is more closely tied to success than cognitive ability.

   Specifically, emotional intelligence (in one of the major models of the term) refers to five distinct abilities that allow human beings to be intelligent on an emotional level. These abilities include emotional awareness, self-regulation, motivation, empathy, and using emotion as a guide for behavior. The idea here is that human beings naturally form connections with one another, often without words, and emotional intelligence is the quality that represents the ability of human beings to do connect effectively on an emotional level.

6. Why is emotional intelligence important in relationships?

   Emotional intelligence is important in relationships for a number of reasons. Emotional intelligence is believed by many psychologists to represent the normal capabilities that human beings use to have normal interactions. Emotional intelligence encompasses the verbal and non-verbal cues that human beings utilize to interact with one another. These cues are clues to the emotional state of the other person and therefore allow us to be "synced" emotionally, which appears to be not only a human characteristic but an animal one.

For example, having empathy for another person first requires that you are able to label what their emotional state accurately. If one is unable to be exercise accuracy in labeling the mental state of another, then one will be unable to share the emotions and experiences of the other. This is really what empathy is: the ability to feel the subjective feelings and emotions that another person feels. Although empathy is only one component of emotional intelligence, it is one that students on the subject can often identify with.

In terms of relationships, emotional intelligence allows you to understand and relate to your significant other without words. Individuals lacking emotional intelligence will be unable to understand their partner in a deep way (including with empathy) and their connection may be flimsy and superficial. Developing emotional intelligence skills can, therefore, be a step towards salvaging a relationship that may be failing.

7. Why do many relationships fail?

Relationships fail for a number of reasons. A relationship may fail because the partners grow apart. A relationship may fail because one partner changes over time and the other does not, so they are no longer equally matched or "right for each other." Some relationships fail because the partners fail to communicate. One partner may be more interested in pursuing their own interests and may behave in a way that is selfish and eventually alienates the other partner.

In truth, some relationships fail because perhaps they were never meant to succeed. Many factors cause couples to pair up, and sometimes people pair up for the wrong reasons. Or perhaps they paired up for a legitimate reason, but that was the only reason and once that cause, such as intense physical attraction, disappeared then there was no longer anything keeping the relationship afloat.

8. Why does it seem that relationships today are more likely to fail than in the past?

It should not come as a surprise that signs of the relationship failure, like divorce rates, are on the rise. And this is not just something happening in the United States, but it can be seen all over the Western world. In fact, the question of why this is happening has been a major issue for social scientists for at least 50 years. There is not a consensus on what the cause is, or whether there is just one cause, but there have been some important observations in psychology that can shed light on the issue.

Narcissistic behavior can be a serious impediment to a relationship. The narcissist is someone who is vain to such a degree that they are unable to care deeply for others and see their own desires and motivations as being paramount. A narcissist may even engage in acts that endanger others because they are so self-centered. It has been argued that some social factors may be causing individuals in the West to behave more narcissistically, which impedes a solid relationship. Also, individuals may be pairing up for the wrong reasons, which will also increase the likelihood that a relationship will fail.

9. Is it possible to salvage my relationship?

    If you are reading this book, it is most likely because you have an interest in trying to save your relationship, or at least to understand why your relationship may be experiencing problems. Every relationship is different, which means that some relationships may have hurdles that can be overcome with the right steps, while others may flounder.

    The purpose of this book is to help you identify the type of relationship you have and to recognize why your relationship may be having problems. Part of this process will involve seriously asking the question of whether or not the relationship can be salvaged. For some of you, the answer may be no. As difficult of a realization as this may be, it is one that must be recognized.

10. What do I do with a partner who does not accept me for who I am?

Acceptance is an important part of any relationship. Indeed, some would argue that acceptance is an essential component of love. That being said, it is not uncommon in many relationships for one partner to attempt to change the other partner. One partner may feel that with a few tweaks here and there their partner may be just the right match for them. In the eyes of the partner seeing to change the other, this is really a matter of making their partner better.

A characteristic of a good relationship is that the members of the partnership make each other better. Making someone better is something that should occur naturally. It is not the same as attempting to change the other person. If we say that acceptance is an important part of a relationship, then a partner who is unable to accept their significant other for who they are may have their own set of problems or perhaps their partner is not right for them. In short, one partner failing to accept the other for who they are is a major red flag.

11. If emotional intelligence is important, does that mean that being more emotional is better for relationships?

There is an important distinction between emotional intelligence and "being emotional." Emotional people are generally thought of as those who act on their own emotions, impulsively, without regard for the other person's emotional state and without going through the process of determining if their emotions are necessary or important in the situation. For example, an important component of emotional intelligence is self-regulation, which means that you can recognize your emotions accurately and halt them or modify them if necessary.

A so-called emotional person does not go through the important emotional self-regulation step. This means that, although they may be engaging in other aspects of emotional intelligence, such as using their emotional awareness as a guide for their behaviors, they are not halting their dysfunctional emotions so they may be behaving in a way more damaging then if they were actually less emotionally aware. This is also true of empathy in which an individual should not only be aware of their own emotional state but should feel the subjective experiences and feelings of the other. Therefore, being more emotional is not necessarily better for relationships if it does not include all aspects of emotional intelligence, including self-regulation and empathy.

12. What are the causes of conflict in a relationship?

The causes of conflict in a romantic relationship are not dissimilar to the causes of conflict in any other relationship or partnership. A power discrepancy that is felt by one partner can be a cause of conflict in a relationship, which can manifest itself in a lack of respect or consideration that one partner feels. If one partner feels that their relationship needs are not being met, this too can be a cause of conflict. Also, if there is a lack of communication in a relationship, conflict can result because the involved individuals do not understand one another or are not seeing eye to eye.

Indeed, some in the psychology field like to approach conflict in a relationship from the standpoint of a need not being met. Just as individuals have their own needs (as individuals), we also have needs in a relationship and if these are not being met, then this can be a cause of unhappiness and conflict. Such unhappiness and conflict can lead to relationship problems that can cause the partnership to fail.

13. Would it help me to see a therapist if I am having relationship problems?

Sometimes it takes an outsider to help people recognize what the problems are in their relationships. It is similar to a business calling in a consultant or an analyst to help them fix their problems. This does not necessarily mean that the problems cannot be fixed without an analyst or a therapist in this example, but sometimes relationship problems can become so entrenched that they cannot be remedied without a third party coming in and using measures to steer the other two parties in the right direction.

For example, if you notice that you and your partner are not on the same page about your relationship, that you and your partner have different assessments of what the problems are, then a therapist can help give an objective assessment of the relationship. Personal feelings can sometimes get in the way of our viewing ourselves, our partners, or our relationships accurately. A therapist might be just what your relationship needs to steer it in the right direction.

14. I have depression and anxiety. How do I know if these problems are impacting my relationship?

Issues of mental health can seriously impact a relationship in a variety of ways, of which one of the more important is that it can impede communication. Mental health issues, like depression and anxiety, can also prevent the normal human bonding mechanism from happening, which means that partners in the relationship are not forming the sorts of connections that they would under normal circumstances.

A good way to illustrate this point is in terms of the normal attachment bond that all human beings form as part of the process of development. Infants have needs, and they become attached to their caregiver by a process that involves how the caregiver responds to the needs of the infant and shows affection. But someone with depression, anxiety, or another mental issue may be unable to respond to an infant appropriately, and therefore, the normal attachment bond does not form as it should. By a similar mechanism, individuals with depression and anxiety may have difficulty interacting with their partner in ways that support or maintain the relationship.

15. Is there an essential problem with marriages and other relationships today that is distinct from the past?

    Many men and women marry for reasons for love or lust and do not recognize that there is generally more to relationships than that, even romantic ones. Such individuals fail to recognize that relationships come with a series of needs for both parties, and that love is just one of those needs. Because there is such a focus on love, men and women in relationships often ignore that their relationships often serve other functions. It is not until these other needs or functions are not being met that people often become aware of them as they pop up in the form of conflicts. For example, a couple may marry for "love", but then they wind up in divorce proceedings when one of the partners loses their employment or source of income.

16. How do I know when it is time to give up on a relationship?

    Everyone wants to save their relationship, but sometimes it is not in the cards. Many people have a sincere interest in putting as much effort into their relationship as they can. They do not want to walk away from a relationship if they believe that it is possible to save it. They may be sincerely attached to the other person - they may care about them - or they may have other reasons why they want the relationship to work, such as financial reasons.

But sometimes, a relationship will fail no matter how much one or both partners want it to work. As you have seen, there are many reasons why relationships do not work out. An important step, therefore, becomes going through a process of analyzing whether or not your relationship has a future. There is no one way to do this, but thinking about whether you and your partners have the same life goals, whether you see eye to eye on important issues, whether you are still attracted to one another as you once were (which does not have to be physical). All of these can clue you in on whether or not your relationship can be salvaged. Do you still love your partner?

17. What are the different types of relationships?

There are many ways to divide relationships into types, but in this book, we use a practical definition that focuses on the salient features of the bond. The following is a list of major relationship types:
- The control relationship
- The open relationship
- The relationship of dependence
- Sexless Relationship

- Long-distance relationship
- Friends with benefits
- Toxic relationships
- Kill time relationship
- Sex only relationship
- Love relationship
- Sacrificial relationship
- Love-hate relationship

18. What is the love-hate relationship?

The love-hate relationship is characterized by strong feelings of love and hate felt by both partners. These relationships are common because of the nature of attraction. The same individual that we may profess to dislike may be the one we are most physically attracted to. There are many factors that play a role in attracting some of which are not well understood. Even what someone smells like, their pheromones can be a cause of strong attraction. There is a thin line between love and hate, and this represents the reality that human beings have emotions and are often guided by them.

Love-hate relationships are problematic. They are problematic because, although love is important for many relationships to endure (romantic or otherwise), most relationships cannot withstand the weight of strong feelings of hate. If one partner in the union truly hates something about the other, then this usually creates a conflict that surfaces in various ways and can only be removed by the termination of the partnership. Ending the partnership can sometimes be difficult because of the great physical attraction that is often present in these relationships, but this can be essential to prevent them from entering into the toxic realm.

19. Is intimacy an essential part of a romantic relationship?

Many people today consider sex an essential component of a romantic relationship. This is because most modern men and women consider love to be critical in any relationship and sex too many people is the most obvious manifestation of love. Intimacy represents love in its most physical form. Intimacy is an easy way to show another person that we love them, and in this sense represents both an animalistic tool and quality and a very human one, one based on decided action.

But intimacy is not necessarily essential to an enduring romantic relationship. Many couples are intimate in the early stages of their relationship, and this intimacy eventually fades, which is not abnormal. Some couples never have intimacy in their relationship, and they can remain married or in stable partnerships for years. A relationship is really about the respective needs of the members being met, and some people have less of a need for intimacy than others.

20. What do I do if I or my partner is lacking in emotional intelligence?

Fortunately for most, EI skills can be acquired. One of the best ways that emotional intelligence skills can be improved is by practicing empathy. This may sound strange, but it essentially means that the individual practices having concern for others and showing this concern. This generally means asking how others are doing and genuinely caring about the answers that they give you. Research suggests that those who practice empathy in this manner eventually come to show empathy spontaneously.

Conclusion

If relationships were easy, every relationship would last forever. What we are seeing is that serious romantic relationships and marriages are more likely to fail than ever before. This truth about today seems strange when we consider that we live in a time in which we are all supposed to be more sensitive to the needs of others and egalitarian. In the workplace, we have learned to be more considerate of others, which may involve not saying or doing things that may hurt or offend others. The same is true at home. Most men and women in a relationship know that they should be sensitive to their partners and regard their partner's wants as just as important as their own.

Why then do we see an increase in relationship failure? Well, understanding this trend requires that we put some thought into what a relationship is. A relationship is an enduring interaction between two people, and it serves a purpose in allowing certain needs to be met. As human beings, we have a need for love, acceptance, safety, and security. We meet many of these needs in a relationship. A relationship also serves other functions like procreation, sexual fulfillment, and emotional connection. Indeed, the formation of romantic relationships is regarded as an essential and normal part of human life.

Of course, the relationship picture is complicated by human behavior and the often individualistic nature of people. Because of this, many different types of relationships can be formed, most with their inherent dysfunctions. We can talk about friends with benefits, dependency and codependency relationships, love-hate relationships. These all represent patterns of relationship problems that represent underlying issues that people have in relating to one another.

Therefore, improving relationships becomes an issue that consists of several steps. These steps include understanding what a good relationship looks like and how your relationship differs, learning the importance of communication in a relationship, making an effort to be more emotionally intelligent, and learning to overcome your fears. For some, taking these steps to improve a relationship involves following tried and tested steps that others have found success with. For some people, the solution may be to go to a therapist. For a few, it may not be possible to salvage the relationship. Fortunately for most of you, salvaging your relationship can be achieved with a little communication. The right kind of communication can go a long way.

Made in the USA
Lexington, KY
17 August 2019